Wooden Spoon Society

RUGBY WORLD '98

EDITED BY

Nigel Starmer-Smith
and Ian Robertson

Queen Anne Press

A QUEEN ANNE PRESS BOOK

© Lennard Associates Limited 1997

First published in 1997 by
Queen Anne Press, a division of
Lennard Associates Limited
Mackerye End
Harpenden, Herts AL5 5DR

A catalogue entry is available from the British Library

ISBN 1 85291 584 6 (paperback)
ISBN 1 85291 583 8 (hardback)

Production Editor: Chris Hawkes
Cover Design/Design Consultant: Paul Cooper
Reproduction: The Colour Edge
Printed and bound in Slovenia

The publishers would like to thank Colorsport for providing most of the
photographs for this book.

The publishers would also like to thank David Gibson of Fotosport;
Sportsfile; and Allsport for providing additional material.

CONTENTS

Wooden Spoon Society – The Charity of British Rugby 5
Spoon at Twickenham (David Roberts) 6

A YEAR AFTER PROFESSIONALISM
Certa amittimus, dum incerta petimus (Paul Stephens) 12
The Impact of Professionalism in:
Wales – And the poor get poorer (David Stewart) 16
Scotland – Rebellion in the air (Alan Lorimer) 18
Ireland – Commonsense or Cuckooland (Sean Diffley) 20
France – The storm is brewing (Chris Thau) 22
Why England U21s? (Clive Woodward) 24

WHERE NOW THE AMATEURS?
What of the Barbarians? (Micky Steele-Bodger) 28
In concordia floriamus – In Friendship We Flourish (Rolph James) 33
Penguin Rugby Club – Life in the Fast Lane (Tony Mason) 36

THE LIONS IN SOUTH AFRICA
Against All Odds (Mick Cleary) 42
The Best of a Bad Job (John Reason) 51
Crossing the Divide (David Lawrenson) 59

RUGBY WORLDWIDE
Fiji Take the World 7s Crown (Ian Robertson) 66
The Glenryk/Henley 7s (Nigel Starmer-Smith) 73
The Biggest Rugby Show on Earth – Two Years and Counting (Chris Thau) .75
England and France in Australia (Kerri Muldoon and Ian Robertson) 79
Other Tours (Bill Mitchell) 83

CLUBS AND CUPS
Sale RFC – Riding High (Geoff Green) 88
Richmond RFC – The Success Formula (Tom Kingston) 93
Thanet RFC – It's Not Over 'Til We Say It's Over (Greg Bayne) 97
Harpenden RFC – Nine Steps to Glory (Michael Parke) 99
Heineken Cup – Here to Stay (John Kennedy) 105
Serevi's Sanyo Success (Nigel Starmer-Smith) 111

PREVIEW OF THE SEASON 1997–98
The Five Nations Championship (Bill McLaren) 116
Key Players 1997–98 (Ian Robertson) 123
The Club Scene (Bill Mitchell, David Stewart, Bill McLaren,
Sean Diffley, Chris Thau) 129
Fixtures 1997–98 147

A Summary of the Season 1996-97 151

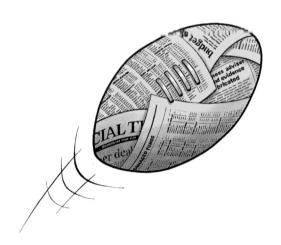

WE ALSO HAVE A PASSION FOR FOOTSIE

We know our way around the FT-SE index and the stock market like others know their way around the rugby pitch. In fact, in the investment field, few are a match for Save & Prosper.

To find out how Save & Prosper can help with your savings and investment plans, call us free on 0800 282 101.

 SAVE & PROSPER

UNIT TRUSTS · PEPS · PENSIONS · BANKING SERVICES

Wooden Spoon Society
- the Charity of British Rugby

Much has happened since the first editorial in the *Wooden Spoon Society Rugby World* book last year in as much that the patronage of the Rugby Football Union has been joined by the patronage of the Scottish Rugby Union, the Welsh Rugby Union, and also the Irish Rugby Football Union.

That in itself would be sufficient to recognise that the Wooden Spoon Society has become 'the charity of British rugby'. However, we were delighted in the spring of 1997 that Her Royal Highness, The Princess Royal, also agreed to become our Royal Patron.

The energy and enthusiasm that Her Royal Highness puts into the game of rugby, in particular north of the border, is the joy of all Scotsmen, the envy of the other Celtic fringe nations and of the might of the English establishment.

This makes us, therefore, doubly pleased that such a Royal Patron should consider the work of the Wooden Spoon Society as deserving of such recognition.

Since our inception, we have recognised that as a charity, our roots are firmly entrenched within the game of rugby football. We have invested much charitable resource into easing the lot of those disadvantaged in life by making their enjoyment of the game and the ethos which surrounds it more pleasurable.

We are, therefore, proud to proclaim that in this year of 1997 we are cementing our relationship with the game, the authorities which control it, the Royal Patron who supports it and, of course, the myriad of club officials, club players and spectators everywhere.

The Wooden Spoon Society is a pro-active event-organising charity which welcomes new members who wish to be part of our growth and our enjoyment.

Full details from the Spoon Office, 81 Middle Wall, Whitstable, Kent CT5 1BW, telephone number: 01227 772295, fax number: 01227 772296.

SPOON AT TWICKENHAM

Billie Williams' cabbage patch is a magical place. From whichever direction you approach Twickenham, there is always a tingle of anticipation, not only at the prospect of the game ahead, but also at the likelihood of meeting old friends in familiar surroundings.

Twickenham has, of course, changed out of all recognition over the last decade and those wonderful old upright stands of the East and the West, that quite magical meeting place on the terrace of the North and the fairly intrusive modern structure of the South, have now given way to a stadium which can hold its own with any other in the world.

But new as it is, it is still a very special place for all lovers of the game of rugby. For Wooden Spoon, Twickenham is indeed a very special home. Over the last few years we have adopted each new structure as it rose from its foundations and have been part of each new facet of the ground as it developed.

Who can forget those long-off days when to attend Twickenham in a wheelchair meant going down to the South East corner in the hope that Paul would not be there that day with his dormobile and its rooftop viewing-platform, because he took up half of the available space.

From the first Wooden Spoon Wheelchair Terrace in the much-loved and much-missed West Stand (so close to the game!), Wooden Spoon has now made its mark upon Twickenham.

We have the two Wooden Spoon bars in the South East and South West wrap-arounds immediately below probably the best viewing area in the ground, the two Wooden Spoon Society wheelchair terraces.

In either wing of the new North stand, there are two other Wooden Spoon bars with counters specially lowered for wheelchair access only.

Our roundels proudly display our association with the Rugby Football Union from the two ground-facing lift shaft walls in the South East and South West corners.

Each match day at Twickenham is a gathering of the clans (if such a Celtic word is not a challenge in itself) and the number of Spoon ties and scarves and hats and shirts that make their appearance at the ground as each match succeeds another, is a tribute to the growth of the charity of British rugby.

The next three pages show graphically what a mark Wooden Spoon has made upon Twickenham and they also equally graphically show the mark that Twickenham has made on the heart of the Wooden Spoon Society.

These photographs were all taken on one day at Twickenham and probably demonstrate better than anything else that the fabric of the ground is also the fabric of Wooden Spoon.

(Far left) The Spoon roundel proudly stands out above the colourful Twickenham crowd, flanked on either side by the Wooden Spoon wheelchair terrace. (Above left and right) No Spoon member need go thirsty at Twickenham where we now have four bars, two in the South East and South West wrap-arounds and two wheelchair counter bars in the North East and North West wrap-arounds.

(Left) The Wooden Spoon Society wheelchair terraces are located in the South West and the South East terraces.

(Far left) Danny Hearn unveils a plaque explaining the re-location of the commemorative stone for the old Wooden Spoon enclosure originally opened by Prince Edward in 1988.

(Above) Barry Wilcher, chief steward of the original Wooden Spoon Society Wheelchair Terrace at Twickenham, returns for another Five Nations match.
(Above right) A Wooden Spoon party hosted by Vauxhall Motors.
(Right) Jerry Guscott hosts the winning team from the Wooden Spoon Society Team Relay Marathon in the British Car Auctions box.

(Far right) In TW1 the Wooden Spoon Rugby World is in great demand, as is the video (right) telling the story of the '71 Lions tour to New Zealand and the way Spoon re-united the Lions last year.

(Far left) Even the stewards at Twickenham wear their Spoon ties on match days.
(Left) Always an early arrival at Twickenham is Colenel Ulton Ryan up from Devon – hopefully no glass containers in that haversack!

(Far middle) In the car park, if you are looking for a sandwich or a cider, look no further than the Spoon Hospitality Volvo.

(Left) The Spoon media team of Ian Robertson, John Inverdale and Alistair Hignell greet Jill and David Roberts from the Spoon office.

performance

from
N E X T

A YEAR AFTER PROFESSIONALISM

CERTA AMITTIMUS, DUM INCERTA PETIMUS

BY PAUL STEPHENS

The summer of 1997 will forever be remembered for two famous victories which brought British and Irish rugby their most meaningful triumphs for more than two decades. Momentous defeats of the Springboks by the Lions, in Cape Town and Durban, will never be forgotten by those who were present or played in them, or by the millions who watched on television. But in fact there were three victories, and the third, a week after the tour to the Rainbow Nation had ended, was every bit as colourful and dramatic as the other two, with almost as much significance.

For Cliff Brittle, re-elected as Chairman of the Board after a stormy AGM, a tough year awaits.

While most would regard the vote for the chairman of the Board of Management at the Rugby Football Union's Annual General Meeting as no more material than having some cabbalistic relevance, the implications of the re-election of Cliff Brittle went far beyond the gilded elegance of the Grand Ballroom at the Hilton Hotel on Park Lane. And, for that matter, well yonder than Twickenham. For Brittle, who invested six weeks of his time persuading the Celtic nations to re-admit England after their brief expulsion from the Five Nations championship, is a devout believer in the purpose of the tournament and an adherent to closer relations between all the participating countries, which is rather more than can be said of those who opposed him, after he was first elected at the RFU's Special General Meeting in January 1996.

Let us be clear about what has happened in the intervening period until the body of the RFU re-convened at the Hilton Hotel for this year's AGM, to observe Brittle's second election triumph. The clubs in membership of the RFU have witnessed not mere organisational solecisms but a money-driven strategy designed to fund the Union's supposed need for money at all costs. The price has been to keep most live international, and all club rugby matches off terrestrial television screens in England at a time when the game at club level needs all the exposure it can get.

Moreover, if one looks at the way the television money from BSkyB is being distributed to the 24 clubs in the new Allied Dunbar Premiership, it can be likened to bankrolling a gambler in the casino of the *Titanic*. When the RFU ought to have shown toughness over a limit to the number of overseas players allowed at each club, they took the most invertebrate line possible. Consequently, we have scores of foreign rejects and has-beens, especially in division one, all earning huge salaries funded by the RFU, which does little for the English game and even less for England-qualified youngsters on the lower rungs of the development ladder.

Not that the two dozen clubs who make up English Rugby Partnership can absolve themselves of any blame in this ruinous process. Sooner or later their rampant cupidity and unbridled self-interest is bound to have painful consequences which their short-sightedness has left them woefully unprepared for. In this, the RFU have shown themselves to be unaware of the first law in the psychology of management, which, as in politics, is about knowing what could happen in the last resort, and being readied for it.

Tony Blair, explaining his vision of a stakeholders' economy, in the days before the General Election, said: 'It isn't about giving power to special interest groups. It is a greater sense of power and partnership. We must give the opportunity for all to prosper, not just a special few. When a small number at the top do well, the rest get left behind. All our people must have a stake in the future.'

Dismiss it as political blather if you like, but perhaps it struck a chord with all those who felt disadvantaged and overlooked in the run-up to this year's AGM, who were also aware that when it comes to reading signals from their core supporters the RFU are illiterate.

Just as John Major's Conservative government was forced to pay the ultimate penalty for losing touch with the electorate, by neglecting the grass-roots element which forms the nucleus of the party and with the Prime Minister failing to distance himself from those whose behaviour had brought the Tories into disrepute, so the RFU deserved their humiliation at the AGM.

For the second time in under two years, the RFU had nominated their preferred candidate for chairman of the Board of Management to oppose Cliff Brittle – this time it was Sussex solicitor Bob Rogers. From the handbill on which Rogers announced his candidature there was a similar worthy call from someone of long and trusted time-serving, such as one would expect to receive from a member seeking re-election to a parish council. There was not a hint of a radical idea in Rogers' message – only a plea for unity and an end to the bitterness.

For those who have long grown tired of reading daily accounts of the personality clashes, rancour and ill-feeling, two aspects of the festering mistrust have remained abundantly clear. Firstly, even by the modest standards of collegiality which have been the rule rather than the exception within RFU committees during this century, the current administration can hardly be judged a happy one in which to serve or from where to preside. Nor has it been one which has discharged its obligations to the most beneficial effect of its widest membership. Secondly, without a commitment to ensure greater accountability, an end to the contemptuous disregard for the wishes of the membership, and an undertaking to put in place vital reforms, Rogers, and those who supported him, had no hope of succeeding.

Much as the debate has been so distressingly personalised, and the RFU have claimed consistently that few of the committee could work with Brittle, this has not been about a simple clash of personalities. Far from it. Sure there have been some big egos and well-preened vanities at the centre of the saga, but essentially it has been about money, a lack of answerability, and the television contracts.

Were one addressing the arguments only at this late stage, there would be an entitlement to ask questions about Brittle's part over the last 20 months or so. After all, he was chairman of the Executive during this period, was he not?

By answering that question it is possible to unearth what lay behind so much of the malevolence and the open hostility to Brittle. From the very beginning of Brittle's period in office he was frustrated by his exclusion from all talks relating to television contracts. He was treated as a *parvenu*. When I asked one RFU committee member about Brittle, the demeaning reply was: 'He's the sort of man who would do a good job on the residents' council at a posh block of flats.' The sneering respondent had conveniently overlooked the fact that Brittle is a self-made millionaire with an impressive commercial track record, and has been involved with the game as a player, coach and administrator for 40 years.

Cliff Brittle had the support of both Lions' manager Fran Cotton (above) and former England captain Bill Beaumont – both of whom were added to the 14-man Board of Management.

The Lions' manager Fran Cotton and former England captain Bill Beaumont were not so easily fooled and they, and many others like Sir Michael Stear, offered Brittle their support at the AGM, where Cotton spoke passionately in favour of Brittle. It did the trick and immediately afterwards Brittle moved to consolidate his position as chairman of the 14-strong Board of Management by adding the names of Beaumont and Cotton to the original 12, while accepting the resignation of one of his arch-opponents, Colin Herridge, the RFU's chairman of finance.

Throughout this turbulent period Brittle has been steadfast in his resolve and true to his beliefs. It is to his great credit that he never lost his dignity in the face of unremitting spitefulness and has subsequently treated his vanquished foes with no unnecessary triumphalism. Well before the effects can be felt of any reforms, Brittle will have to keep his nerve while Judge Gerald Butler delivers his judicial inquiry into the affairs and running of the Union.

'I have promised Judge Butler my fullest cooperation,' said Brittle. 'But people must remember, I've been fighting the whole of the RFU machinery. It's been a long battle, but I hope now that the fighting and unpleasantness will end and we can get down to the important business of making the changes which will benefit all in the game.

'There are a number of things I'm not happy with. I'm not content with the structured season. We need to look at a template for each level. I want to re-establish a harmonious relationship with the other European countries. I think now that some of the division one clubs realise they have a problem with too many overseas players on their books, and we must address this issue.

'The television question is altogether more difficult. As I had no part in the negotiations there is very little which can be done in the short term. The RFU is contractually bound by decisions made without my knowledge.'

The nugget of doubt over allegations of graft and impropriety within the RFU, which relates almost exclusively to the television arrangements, could become a boulder unless and until they are properly substantiated. It is hoped that Judge Butler will explore every avenue of uncertainty where these charges are concerned, before declaring them unfounded. Any lack of resolution in this regard could have consequences too awful to contemplate.

The outgoing RFU president John Richardson, who has no right to be more kindly remembered than either of his two predecessors, Bill Bishop or Dennis Easby, should at least be congratulated for setting up the Butler Inquiry. Let us hope it does its work well.

Unfortunately, Richardson cannot be excused or forgiven for endorsing the arrangement which comes into being this winter when, for the first time, some Five Nations championship matches will be played on Sundays.

This is another television-led example of change being made without any thought being given to the true followers of the game whose enjoyment of international rugby is complemented by the social nature of winter weekends in Cardiff, Edinburgh, Dublin and Paris. The leisurely journey home after a Saturday night's excess will soon be a thing of the past, to be replaced by a mad Sunday-evening rush to get back in time for work on Monday morning. Otherwise it will mean taking an extra day's holiday. It is a change for the sake of change and television's even bigger purse of loose change.

'This is another situation I have inherited,' said Brittle. 'Of course we want to see all Five Nations games televised, though my preference has always been for staggered kick-off times on Saturdays.'

As Cliff Brittle wrestles with the almost impossibly difficult problems he will undoubtedly face as the most powerful man in English rugby and guardian of the game's traditions – while disparate interest groups, television companies and club owners continually cry out for change – it is our duty to remind him of the words of Plautus: *Certa amittimus, dum incerta petimus*, 'We lose what is certain, while we pursue uncertainties.'

The outgoing RFU president John Richardson (pictured second from the right) must be congratulated on the setting up of the Butler inquiry, which will look into television arrangements – a problem which could have major consequences for the game.

THE IMPACT OF PROFESSIONALISM

WALES – And the poor get poorer

BY DAVID STEWART

The editors asked for a piece on the impact of professionalism in the Welsh game. The request arrived on the day Cardiff took the Welsh Rugby Union to the High Court, which rather speaks for itself. On the face of it, that battle is whether the Union can compulsorily take a 'golden share' from each of the senior Welsh clubs in return for the monies they distribute, generated largely from the television contracts for competitions in which the clubs play. The bigger picture relates to the independence of the largest clubs as the professional game develops, including the freedom to play in whatever structure and competitions they wish. Ultimately, this could mean one or more of Wales' best clubs playing outside the auspices of the WRU. For reasons not unconnected with relative poverty, all the other senior clubs bar Ebbw Vale and Newport fell into line with the Union.

Players have, of course, been paid in Wales for many years. A biography of the great Tony O'Reilly records that as a student in the mid 1950s Cliff Morgan would arrange for him to play a series of invitational games each September around the clubs of Wales. For each and every one he would charge expenses from Galway – the furthest point away in Ireland – and the resulting funds would see him through the remainder of the academic year! The difference between then, the intervening period of brown envelopes and boot money, and now, is that the sums demanded and being paid are no longer affordable.

As chairman of the Welsh Union, difficult times lie in waiting for the man who took Rugby Union into the professional era – Vernon Pugh.

There is not enough money in the game. Teams are not good enough, the product neither sufficiently attractive nor well enough marketed, and many clubs have become over committed. Most of the Welsh first and second divisions are probably technically insolvent. A Welshman, Vernon Pugh, led the game into professionalism as chair of the International Board. Some suggest the domestic backdrop left little alternative, what with the Inland Revenue asking increasingly difficult questions and so on. Having uncorked the professional bottle the same Pugh now stands accused as chairman of the Union, of trying to force the genie back in via the 'golden share' and other proposals.

What has changed already? Naturally the demands on coaches and committees are greater. Many volunteers have simply given up and slipped away. The larger clubs have formally moved over to corporate status with Boards of Directors and a professional administration. The largest club, Cardiff, has gone for a full-scale public share issue. Llanelli plan to follow suit, having entered a sale-and-lease-back arrangement for their ground to clear mounting debts. Player movement has slowed because people are now contractually tied.

The game in Wales must find its natural level, namely one that is economically viable. Not many will be fully professional, some will be semi-pro, more still will be expenses only and at the bottom end, the amateur game will continue where people actually pay for the privilege of playing! Developments will probably follow those in soccer and cricket earlier this century.

What will happen at the top end? Wales does not have the commercial base of the larger English cities. Only Cardiff would have a business life remotely similar to Newcastle, Manchester, Birmingham or Leeds – each of who can viably support at least one large club – and London perhaps three or four. Leicester and Bath presently flourish on the back of their playing excellence but traditional areas such as Bristol and Gloucester may be off the pace. Which way will the great old West Walian clubs of Swansea, Llanelli and Neath go? Arguably only one will survive at the very highest level. Is a WRU-inspired merger an option, to ensure a centre of excellence in West Wales? Inevitably it seems television money, probably from satellite, will dominate future finance below international level. In less than five years from now, might there be an all-European league, with live matches broadcast as with Premiership soccer, up to five nights a week? It is that prospect which focuses minds and is at the centre of the club versus union dispute. For the health of the international game in Wales it is essential the country is competitively represented at the highest level of the new era.

The shadow of the Welsh soccer clubs is a discomforting one – only three clubs out of 92 in the Football League, and poor relations at that. The prospect of top-level rugby disappearing from places like the Scottish Borders, the Gwent Valleys, Mid Glamorgan and West Wales will dishearten all those who value what these areas have given to the game's history, but the threat is a very real one. Without vast injections of capital from so-far unidentified sources, it is not easy to detect another outcome.

We now await the building of the Millennium Stadium for the 1999 World Cup final. When the ground was last redeveloped, it was done in such a way as to enable internationals to continue to be played in Cardiff. Not this time. Everyone is off to Wembley, or will they? There is a possibility of Welsh teams in the next two seasons playing in stadiums either half empty or with a minority of their own fans. At the end of 1996, Australia and South Africa played in Cardiff, on Sundays, two weeks apart. Despite a television and poster advertising campaign, the Union could not fill the stadium on either occasion. A fall off of interest in the game, particularly amongst the younger generation, is detectable. Junior clubs that used to run four sides now run three. Have we seen the end of the big tours? Cardiff, Newport and Llanelli have all beaten the All Blacks. They may well never have another chance.

The New Zealanders and Australians have shown us the way, in that the entire organisation of their domestic rugby is geared towards giving their national side the best possible chance of success. The WRU would like to follow a similar path, but the way in which professionalism has taken root in England and Wales, based around the clubs, is making that difficult and has led directly to battles in both the boardroom and in the courts. How the picture will look by the turn of the century is very difficult to assess, the only certainty being a rocky path from here to there with a number of casualties along the way.

SCOTLAND – Rebellion in the Air

BY ALAN LORIMER

Financial prudence has always been a Scottish characteristic. And no less so in the Scots' approach to confronting the problems of rugby's new professional era. Canniness, it seems, has kept the lid on a potentially troublesome pot which elsewhere has blown its top in dramatic ways.

The Scottish Rugby Union's priority was to stem what seemed a potentially large flow of players south of the border. The signs were already there when international players, Doddie Weir and Gary Armstrong signed for Newcastle and Craig Joiner joined Leicester for reputedly large fees.

The kind of backer who had pumped cash into the leading English clubs was simply not to be found north of the border. Club rugby in Scotland, despite attempts by several prominent individuals to talk up its commercial viability, was to remain a poor cousin of its English relative. Professionalism in Scotland, it seemed, was not to be market led. For the Scots, a central solution had to be found.

The SRU was not slow in appreciating this fact and consequently moved quickly to sign up an initial batch of some 40 leading players. These players were offered either full-time or part-time contracts worth between £20,000 and £50,000 a year depending on the worth of the individual player.

These sums represented retainer salaries. Additional match fees and a win bonus scheme covering the district championship, the Heineken Cup and Conference, and all the different grades of Scotland representative rugby were paid as part of the deal.

In one quick swoop the SRU had achieved control over the leading players and in so doing had side-stepped a similar power struggle to the one that threatened to tear the game apart in England.

This was necessary to implement the SRU's survival plan on the playing side. In their document *Strategy for Success in the Open Future*, the SRU stated, 'The demands of the open game mean that players must become full-time professionals to develop to their potential and to compete with the best in the world.

'That degree of full-time professionalism cannot be met a club level in Scotland and .... can only realistically and effectively be developed at district level.'

The decision had been made. Scotland's future lay in the district route and not, as in England, through strong clubs. The contracted players would form part of a professional district set-up run along similar lines to the Australian and New Zealand systems.

The mandate to pursue this route had been virtually granted six months earlier at an extraordinary meeting of the Scottish Rugby Union in February 1996 when the SRU, with a huge backing from member clubs, won its case for districts rather than clubs to represent Scotland in the Heineken Cup.

A number of leading clubs, however, were not at all happy with the district route. Their power and influence was being eroded sharply. There seemed an unfairness in what the SRU had done. Rebellion was in the air.

The up-shot was the formation of a leading club's association (SFDR) and the appointment of an influential chairman John MacKay, who had formerly headed the Post Office in Scotland. Talks with, and advice from the likes of Sir John Hall, Peter Wheeler and Gareth Jones, undoubtedly boosted the confidence of the new association, but the real power lay with the SRU. Nothing was going to shift Murrayfield's resolve.

Meanwhile the SRU had embraced the professional era in a number of other ways, the most significant being a restructuring of their administration. The amateur committee-based systems were still retained, but into the SRU came a new breed of cat with the commercial acumen to ensure that what had become a multi-million pound business was to stay in functional shape.

Men like Malcolm Murray, the chief general manager of Scottish Life, George Mathewson, the chief executive of the Royal Bank of Scotland and Sir William Purves of the Hongkong and Shanghai Banking Corporation were absorbed into the SRU to give expert financial advice.

Significantly, too, the old structure run by long-serving committee men, while still remaining in place, was radically remodelled to allow the decision-making of a modern business to be conducted on a day-to-day basis by experts.

The SRU also recruited the services of Rangers chairman David Murray, whose success at Ibrox, it was hoped, could fire up profits at Murrayfield and brought in former stars John Jeffrey and Andy Irvine to add guidance.

What impact all the effects of professionalism have had on the playing side is difficult to assess. Arguably, so great has been the change that there has not yet been time for it to work through to player level. Certainly last season – one of Scotland's poorest Five Nations championships for a number of years – would suggest that the SRU did not get its money's worth from the players.

But to make a snap judgement on the basis of one season would be unfair. It will take time for the district professional scene to bed in and equally so for professionalism to work at national level. Particularly so for a country that has had no experience of 'shamateurism'.

Former Scotland stars Andy Irvine and John Jeffrey have been brought in to help the SRU's drive to increase profits.

As for club rugby, the SRU, awash with the new wealth from re-negotiated television fees, initiated an accreditation scheme whereby clubs could apply for grants to fund professional coaches, fitness advisors and administrators – a recognition that it is clubs who will be the main providers of Scotland's future professionals.

The trick, it seems, in all this massive metamorphosis, is in simultaneously managing the professional and the amateur game. In Scotland the amateur game will carry on at club level, the professional side of rugby will operate at district level and above.

If the two can co-exist then rugby's administrators will have achieved success where other sports have failed. But the real measure of how well the shift to professionalism has been managed north of the border will be on the playing field. 1999, indeed, will be an important World Cup for Scotland.

IRELAND – Commonsense or Cuckooland?

BY SEAN DIFFLEY

The Irish Rugby Football Union's annual meeting in June, at the end of the first year of professionalism, was quite upbeat. Even if the generous overtures towards the leading players were not exactly being greeted with many signs of enthusiasm, the outgoing president Bobby Deacy said he was convinced 'the tide was turning'.

Not alone were the England-based players failing to respond to the offers of well-endowed contracts, the signs were that other young players were more anxious to embrace the streets of the UK paved with gold. Despite Mr Deacy's optimism, the turning tide still seemed to be far out on the Irish Sea.

An Irish squad had been chosen and up to 40 players were offered contracts of a basic £70,000, which with houses and all sorts of extras would not fall much short of £100,000. The proviso was that they should reside in Ireland and play for an Irish club in the All Ireland League and be available for their provincial team in the European competitions.

The silence from the cross-channel based players was deafening. Whilst it was said that the various agents were talking to the IRFU, the various asides were having it that the players were not all that impressed and felt that domestic Irish rugby was not the place to exhibit their wares to the best effect.

So why were the IRFU confident that the changes were coming and that the leading players would, sooner rather than later, return to the domestic fold?

Officialdom believes that the financial set-ups of many of the big professional clubs in England are not viable.

Tom Kiernan pointed out that it is reckoned that it costs £1.5 million to finance a professional club for a season. And his fellow International Board member Syd Millar also felt that some clubs have over-committed themselves financially and that the foundations, consequently, were in danger of collapsing.

International Board member Syd Millar remains convinced that the northern hemisphere is coping better with the advent of professionalism than its southern counterpart.

Millar also made the interesting observation that, contrary to the general view, the southern hemisphere was not ahead of the north in coping with the new professional era. 'They weren't ready for it at all,' claimed Millar. 'We who opposed the whole idea are coping much better.'

The Union believes that the Irish structure of club, province and national side is the proper one and they believe that committed provincial participation in the Heineken Cup is essential for the future of Irish rugby. A few weeks later, the IRFU announced contracts for provincial home-based players. Each provincial management was allowed to nominate 30 players and the IRFU opened the proceedings with initial offers to 76 players from Leinster, Ulster, Munster and Connacht. Full-time players – and there were 12 on the list – were offered a £25,000 retainer fee, plus a bonus offer of £500 for a win in the Heineken Cup or Conference. The part-timers were offered £7,500 plus the bonuses.

The only really notable players on the long list who were offered the full-time contract were Mick Galwey and Anthony Foley, both recent internationals.

Certainly the IRFU have made clear that they are willing to spend the money even if their commitments are large, including the £100 million that will be required to finance a new stadium, either to replace on a green site, or to re-mould Lansdowne Road itself.

The bottom line on that is that it is the Five Nations championship that finances all the works and pomps of the IRFU and Irish Rugby. In that regard the annual IRFU meeting made a special point of thanking Millar, Kiernan and Vernon Pugh for 'saving the Five Nations last season'.

Lansdowne Road yields well over £2 million for each Five Nations match, a tidy sum which enables the IRFU to run the game and also to build up its handy little sum of more than £15 million in investments. And up to last season, the first professional season, the annual operating surplus for all its activities amounted to more than £1.5 million each year. But last season players had to be paid and the operating surplus shrunk down to just over a quarter of a million pounds.

So the importance of the Five Nations is obvious, as is the importance of doing well in that annual tournament. Recent experience has been pretty shattering and the fervent hope is that Brian Ashton will arrest recent trends where most of Ireland's opponents beat them, often by record scores.

Ashton arrived too late on the scene last season to do much about changing things and he had a tough summer assignment in New Zealand and Western Samoa with an Irish Development side which experienced the chasm that divides the respective standards of play. Ashton's main task as he prepares for a new season is to throw off all the old baggage, mainly official, and pursue his own course.

We will have one onerous task of assembling a squad, almost all of whom live and play their football in England. And he could well ponder why Ian McGeechan and Jim Telfer were able to inspire such fine performances with the Lions in South Africa from Jeremy Davidson, Paul Wallace, Keith Wood and Eric Miller – performances which amazed Irish followers. It all rather underlines the theory of some that Ireland does not lack talent and ability among its players, but that it is not properly harnessed by those whose responsibility it is to select and motivate. The big question is, 'Can Ashton do a better job?'Or, as some fear, will he be allowed?

And the really big question – is Irish rugby living in cloud cuckooland, believing it can survive relatively unblemished in the new professional era? Or is the IRFU right in believing that it is others who are living in a financial Never Never Land and that with the advent of commonsense, everything in the garden will grow bright again?

Brian Ashton's arrival on the international scene did little to change things for Ireland, but it is hoped that his influence will start to prevail in the coming season.

FRANCE – The storm is brewing

BY CHRIS THAU

On the surface, the transition from amateurism to professionalism has not had much of an impact on French rugby, although several well-publicised *contretemps* between players, clubs and the FFR have been recorded. The first division clubs, the so-called élite clubs, formed an organisation which, after a fairly long and painful arm-wrestling contest, was recognised by the FFR and integrated into the official set-up as the Commission National de Rugby d'Elite (CNRE). Meanwhile, concerned by the progress of the wealthy 20, the second and third division clubs formed another organisation, Amicale de Clubs de Rugby Français (ACRF) which was also recognised by the FFR and used as a bargaining chip in the negotiations with the CNRE.

Castres offered Thomas Castaignède a tempting package to prevent him from pursuing his rugby career in England.

However, other than political posturing and blood-letting, it was business as usual – in other words, money changed hands, players changed clubs, clubs fiddled the books, France won the Five Nations and Toulouse won the championship. After all, the cynics say, French rugby did not turn professional in August 1995, it declared itself an 'open' game – meaning it is neither amateur nor professional. This is a historic ambiguity and has conditioned the development of French rugby since time began What it meant, was that the players were always going to be paid for playing, which has been accepted as legitimate, but that payment was not going to be the only reward.

What the French clubs did, with great understanding and unquestionable vision, was to manufacture 'packages' (money and professional opportunities) for the players it targeted. This is why Thomas Castaignède turned down a very tempting offer from England, for a 'package' from Castres, which takes into account his future professional career as well. In other words, Castaignède has the cake and eats it, which may not be as bad as its sounds. This is perhaps what is missing in the British game, 'professionalised' overnight, without too much thought or concern for the players' future.

Within this context is it worth pointing out that none of the current internationals (the Grand Slam team) have left France. The French stars to have crossed *La Manche*, are either out of favour – Benezech the 'Red Robbo' of the French team – or at the end of an illustrious career – Cabannes and Sella – ready to capitalise on the cash available in Britain. Saint-André's decision to join Gloucester, and Roumat's announcement that he was going 'to become a professional rugby player' – as if until now his profession had prevented him from concentrating 100 per cent on his rugby career – must be seen within the same context.

This apparent ambiguity explains why in France the changeover appeared reasonably well-managed compared to events in Britain, where professionalism has had such a traumatic impact on the structure of the game. But beneath this surface of calm and tranquillity a storm is brewing. While most of the clubs went on paying their players in cash, under the table, the clubs' wages bill, forced up by the emergence of a highly inflated international players' market, soared, threatening the stability, and in some cases the very existence, of several French clubs.

Lourdes RC, the great club of Jean and Maurice Prat, is heavily in debt and its president Monsieur Kneabel resigned. Vienne CS is torn apart by a major scandal, with its former president Jean Claude Nuvollini accused of financial mismanagement, while neighbouring Valence is insolvent. Racing CF has had to reduce the wages of its leading players, while Grenoble is nearly a quarter of a million francs in the red.

Argèles-sur-Mer, an ambitious club in Languedoc, won the right to play among the élite 20 when they beat Nice last season. But the Mayor, former international Jean Carrère, failed in his attempt to raise the funds to support the club in the élite first division this season. As a consequence, Argèles renounced promotion and amalgamated with St Cyprien in the second division.

Laurent Cabannes in action for Harlequins against Gloucester. Last season saw an influx of French players into the English leagues.

The misfortune of Argèles was the luck of Nice, with the local City Hall ready to invest £350,000 to keep the rugby club afloat. Toulon was threatened with closure by the FFR, unless a solution to cover its £400,000 debt was found. The City Hall and the Regional Council have agreed to cover two-thirds of the debt.

In a recent interview Dax president, former French fly half Jean-Louis Berot, warned that the game was about to run out of control. 'Are we professionals or not? This is the question. To be honest, French rugby is unable to pay its professionals a decent salary, similar to soccer and basketball. Rugby cannot afford it. Paris Saint Germain (soccer team) have a budget of £35 million, Pau-Orthez, the basketball team, have £5.5 million, while our wealthiest clubs have a budget of £1.5 million. We cannot compete. The tragedy is that some fools have launched French rugby into this inflationary spiral which could have disastrous consequences.'

Although no club owners in the mould of Nigel Wray or Sir John Hall have emerged in French rugby, clubs of the likes of Castres and Stade Français-CASG are 'owner's clubs' in everything but name. Wealthy benefactors, such as media-magnate Max Gauzzini the multi-millionaire Stade Français president, are the inflationary factors in French rugby. Money is no object at Stade Français. The club president spent a fortune on recruiting new players, having already spent hundreds of thousands of pounds the previous season to secure a place among the top 20. I have very little doubt that having succeeded in gaining a place among the élite 20, Stade Français will be in the top four this season. However, for every successful Stade Français, there will be an Argèles-sur-Mer.

WHY UNDER 21s?

BY **CLIVE WOODWARD**

The 'fall-out' caused by the game becoming fully professional has covered many areas of the sport, from management, to players, to ticket prices! One area that is of direct interest to me is that of the Under 21s. The many changes that have taken place have already hit the development of younger players hard. There are several reasons for this.

Understandably, due to the pressure of sustained success, coaches are looking ever further for better, more accomplished and more experienced players. The problem arises when many of these players are foreign imports. They have fulfilled their ambitions to play for their respective countries and are now looking for experience elsewhere or to earn some money before the end of their illustrious careers. This one area alone has had a direct knock-on effect. As clubs are forced into buying 'instant success' as well as having to cope with the length of the season, which is full of highly competitive games and vital fixtures, they are less likely to be keen to give the young 19- or 20-year-olds a break in the big game. So where are these promising young players going to gain experience?

England U21s in action against Scotland. The Under 21 internationals are now played alongside the senior fixtures to add more importance and relevance.

Top clubs are in a dilemma. They want to develop young talent, but have to gain valuable points from their matches. Inevitably, many youngsters are the backbone of the development squads and the second teams. So when will these players have the chance to become major decision-makers, and learn to dictate play on a regular basis at a highly competitive and meaningful level? Several do feature in senior sides, but all too often they find themselves out of the major decision-making positions. With today's pressures, it takes a lot of courage in mid-week selection to give a young player the opportunity to become a major play-maker. It's hard to imagine where future England stars are going to emerge from if this trend were to continue.

I'm not saying that foreign players must not be welcomed at club level, they add spice, entertainment and more interest for players, coaches and spectators alike – clubs must be allowed to recruit as they please – but we need to look at the development of future England sides.

Changes were made to the set-up of the U21s last season. For all of the reasons previously discussed, divisional rugby has now become a crucial element in identifying young talent. It enables players, not yet physically able to cope with the demands of first-team rugby, to be exposed to rugby of a higher representative standard than their weekly menu of second-team or development-squad rugby. Whereas in the past the national U21 sides have liaised with senior divisional sides, they are now working closely and directly with the divisional U21 sides. The whole idea being to identify this valuable pool of talent early and fast track them within the divisional and national squads. Through much more competitive game situations at divisional and national level, we can ensure that these players gain the necessary experience of the 'big' game, encouraging them to become decision- and play-makers. It takes time to insert *the* most essential element into their game – confidence. They will undoubtedly gain this by playing competitive fixtures on a regular basis for divisional and national U21 sides.

Obviously clubs would be opposed to their promising young players spending too much time away, no one wants to over-play young players either, and so country commitments on top of club and divisional games need to be examined. On the other hand, look at what the clubs stand to gain through the experience that the players would receive. Many of the top club's objections would be answered with a little reorganisation.

1: Representative games need to be played wherever possible within a four- to six-week period.

2: The players must be coached by some of the best available, both at international level and divisional level. And they don't come much better than Rob Smith or Andy Robinson!

3: The four divisions need to approach coaching in the same vein – perhaps bringing in experienced players of the calibre of Dean Richards, Rory Underwood or Brian Moore.

4: Games need to be meaningful and of a highly competitive nature.

The four national U21 divisions along with the England selection and management have worked together closely and are already forging the way ahead for still closer links. U21 Internationals are now played alongside the senior fixtures, adding importance and relevance to the games. The sides train together at Bisham Abbey, giving the younger player more confidence and making him more accustomed to the atmosphere of the national side should his big chance come. The 1996–97 U21 season culminates with a tour of Australia, including highly competitive fixtures and a demanding training schedule. All of this can only serve to enhance young-player development to the benefit of their clubs. It is in everyone's best interests, especially that of a future England side, to support the momentum behind the development of U21 rugby. Although it has been an exciting season with many innovations, there is still more to do. Only by investing now in the enormous wealth of young talent that we undoubtedly possess, can we ensure future success at international level. The coming season shows great promise, as all four divisions will play the touring All Black U21 side followed by an international fixture – an ideal way to move forwards.

HEINZ
MEANZ
TRIEZ

A GREAT SUPPORTER OF WORLD RUGBY

WHERE NOW THE AMATEURS?

WHAT OF THE BARBARIANS?

BY **MICKY STEELE-BODGER**

It was at the International Board Meeting in Paris in August 1995 that the decision was taken to make the game 'open' and to accept professionalism. It is not surprising that the rights and wrongs of that decision and as to how it has been implemented are still a matter of debate, for the impact on the game in these islands has been massive.

A month later there was a conference held at Twickenham at which Will Carling, then the England captain, said that in his opinion professionalism would threaten the future of Lions tours and also the Barbarians, even though the first Lions tour was in 1888 and the Barbarians were founded two years later. Well, the Lions have given their answer through winning the series against South Africa, but what of the Barbarians?

In the season prior to the advent of professionalism, the Barbarians had their regular fixtures with Newport, East Midlands, Leicester and Cardiff and in addition, Stirling County – the latter three clubs at the time being their respective national league champions. In May, the club was invited to play Ireland in what was termed 'The Peace International' at Lansdowne Road, a ground where 18 months earlier the club had also defeated South Africa. Following Ireland, an invitation was accepted to undertake a short tour to Japan in aid of the Kobe Earthquake Disaster Fund and also to play a match

Philippe Saint-André dives over the line during the Barbarians victory over the South African tourists in 1995.

Dean Richards charges at the Irish defence during the Peace International at Lansdowne Road.

against Scotland in support of those most affected by the Dunblane School tragedy. Sadly such terrible events do occur, but we felt privileged to be asked to help in such good causes.

Those were international occasions and the response was heart-warming. The advent of professionalism, however, has brought with it contracts binding players to their union or their club and also an intensification of national league programmes as clubs strive for the success necessary to ensure continuing high-level sponsorship or to attract large capital investments by interested individuals. The wages of players are such that help from a source outside the club is essential – it also means that it is necessary for the players to be covered by insurance for any loss of earnings following injury. As their contracts are not with the Barbarians, separate policies are required and must be effected.

With the game still in some turmoil and the structure of the season ever changing, it has meant that traditional dates have had to alter and, last season, our Boxing Day match with Leicester was played in February. Changes are also occurring in the pattern of touring – the major unions are trying to visit the British Isles more frequently and play far fewer matches, most of them internationals. However, in 1998 we hope to be

awarded our traditional fixture and play the Springboks, against whom our record is 2–2.

I have mentioned some of the problems, but there are many pluses as well. Invitations from clubs are regularly received and there is no doubt that if the traditional opponents cannot continue then there are replacements only too willing to step in.

In our Centenary year, Scottish Amicable became the Barbarian Club's first sponsor – their support has been sincere and generous and the name 'Amicable' seems most appropriate.

In the 1990s the decision was made to undertake short overseas tours and so far the Barbarians have been to Russia in 1992, Zimbabwe in 1994, Japan in 1996, and Italy in 1997 – the Club has also been invited to Argentina in 1998. Undoubtedly, there is a need for such tours and this programme will continue.

The French Barbarians club has instituted, in cooperation with Air France, the Paris 7s tournament and we intend to support our French counterparts by entering the tournament annually. The club was also invited to participate in the Middlesex 7s and the tournament was won convincingly with a squad consisting of players from England, Fiji, Scotland and Wales.

Clubs are under pressure on many sides, but they have been remarkably generous and understanding in releasing players appreciating, as they do, their aspirations. It is, however, the players themselves who hold the key and they are very keen, in fact often asking, to play for the club and as long as that is the picture, there can be no doubting its future.

(Previous page) All in a good cause as Aaron Pene takes on the Scottish defence in the match organised to help those most affected by the Dunblane tragedy. (Below) David Campese in the traditional end of tour fixture for touring sides.

GORY, BLOOD-SOAKED COMBAT BETWEEN MONSTERS, FREAKS AND HIDEOUSLY DEFORMED BEASTS.

(NO IT'S NOT SATURDAY AFTERNOON AT THE STOOP.)

Tackle the very latest in hi-tech attractions in The Adrenalin Zone at the Trocadero. Segaworld, Virtual World, Virtual Glider, Showscan's Emaginator, Funland and Lazer Bowl. And after you've finished rucking and mauling with them you can always try Madame Tussaud's Rock Circus, Thunder Drive or Planet Hollywood. So you can see how a visit to the Trocadero kicks all other days out into touch.

No.1 PICCADILLY CIRCUS, LONDON. TELEPHONE: 0171 439 1791.

IN CONCORDIA FLOREAMUS
– In Friendship We Flourish

BY BRIGADIER ROLPH JAMES

The Public School Wanderers club was formed in 1940 by Charles Burton, a Fleet Street journalist. It was originally formed to provide cricket and rugby for public schoolboys on vacation, but with difficulties arising from wartime fixtures, the club took on a new role of providing games for both schoolboys and servicemen. During the period of hostilities the club provided over a thousand games of cricket and rugby for servicemen from all parts of the commonwealth.

After the war, the club became open by invitation and whilst retaining its tradition of playing a minimum of 514 games against public schools, the fixtures list became stronger with the years. Today, the club's fixtures embrace the full spectrum of rugby activity – playing regional fixtures and celebration games such as opening of new club houses, providing teams to play in developing rugby countries, engaging in other missionary activities and, of course, playing those school games. International fixtures with Belgium, Germany, Netherlands, Italy, Korea, Kenya and New Zealand are but a few of the other commitments the Wanderers have undertaken.

The Public School Wanderers side to tour Zimbabwe in 1975 contained many familiar faces – most of whom went on to represent their respective countries.

Since its foundation, over 2,000 players have represented the Wanderers in over 5,000 matches. The Wanderers continue to receive many invitations from the world of rugby not all of which, regrettably, it is possible to accept.

Notable events in the history of the Wanderers include fielding a team comprising 15 internationals early in the 1988–89 season against the redoubtable Bath side who also had a full complement of internationals. Bath were the first club since Newport in 1902 to achieve this feat. This game was in aid of the Wishing Well Appeal for Great Ormond Street Children's Hospital. Those present witnessed a veritable feast of rugby.

In past seasons, the Public Schools Wanderers have represented the RFU at the German Rugby Federation Centenary, and have also toured in East Africa, South Africa, America, Canada, Bermuda, Argentina, Uruguay and most European countries. In 1989 the team visited Pebble Beach, California, and took part in the Monterey Tournament as well as playing against the Eagles, the Pelicans and the Grizzlies – formidable opposition as their names imply. Perhaps the club's greatest achievement was in June 1982 when, with only two weeks' notice, they took over the British Lions' cancelled fixtures in Zimbabwe and the touring party, captained by Fergus Slattery, boasted 18 internationals, including nine former British Lions, three of whom later joined the Lions' tour of South Africa. In 1986, the Wanderers returned to Zimbabwe and completed an undefeated tour including matches against the national team.

It is, however, in 7s tournaments that the Wanderers have probably etched their worldwide reputation. They have been finalists on two occasions in the Middlesex 7s, have represented England in the Monte Carlo 7s in 1987, 1988 and 1989, being winners in that year, and were also finalists in the Hong Kong 7s in 1986 narrowly beaten by Australia. However, the Wanderers had beaten New Zealand in the semi-final! The Wanderers have also been London 7s winners, and more recently they were winners of the 1996 African Safari 7s. They were semi-finalists and plate winners of the same tournament in 1997.

Nevertheless , the success of the Wanderers club is not measured in its victories, but more in its established tradition of playing entertaining rugby. A player is invited to become a Wanderer because he is a credit to the game and will enter into the spirit of maintaining the high standards of play achieved by the generations of preceding club members.

The international line-up of the Public School Wanderers side that took on Bath in 1988–89.

The Hong Kong 7s has proved to be a happy hunting ground for the Wanderers. Pictured is the 198? squad led by Scotland's John Jeffreys.

Charles Burton recognised, even in the early days, the ever-increasing demands on the players and the need to create the opportunity for players to display their natural flair. These opportunities are no less relevant in 1997 than they were in 1940. Whilst the basic philosophy of the Wanderers club has not changed, the club itself has evolved to meet the significant developments in Rugby Union. The Wanderers have refocused their fixture list to reflect the realities of the modern professional rugby era and recognise the contactual obligations that players now have to their clubs. Fortunately clubs still enjoy the more relaxed games that the Wanderers offer and use them to test players recovering from injury, and to give opportunities to younger players to deliver in a broader arena. In many respects the Wanderers are returning to their grass roots – a combination of youth and experience. The Millenium is faced with optimism. There are over 2,000 clubs in England alone, most of which subscribe to the Wanderers' philosophy. Many former Wanderers players now occupy an influential part in the new rugby régime. They have brought with them not just the obvious skills of administration, but undoubtedly will reflect the ethics of the Wanderers club.

Although nomadic by definition, the club's roots are deep. The Wanderers' players list over the years includes representatives from almost all major rugby-playing nations.

In the increasingly competitive world of sponsorship with its commercial imperatives, the Wanderers have continued to enjoy the benefit of a loyal and supportive group of sponsors, both vice-presidents and corporate. This has provided a reasonable financial base from which the club's playing commitments can be realised.

In a sport where the players, the referees, and the administrators are all inter-dependent the club continues to be honoured by the considerable support of all – *in concordia floreamus*.

PENGUIN RUGBY CLUB –
Life in the fast lane

BY **TONY MASON**

In 1959 at Sidcup Rugby Club, Tony Mason and Alan Wright were two young enthusiastic rugby players – well, one was young, one not so young – and the older one was involved in organising a rugby tour to Berlin for Easter 1958. When it was discovered that the venue was in East Berlin, Colonel Prentice, the then secretary of the Rugby Union blew a gasket and promptly cancelled the tour as contact with any form of communism was *verboten* – almost under penalty of death. This left the older player with a squad of players with nowhere to go, but still keen to go somewhere. So he set about finding somewhere to go and enlisted the help of the younger player, who was like-minded in his rugby outlook. Copenhagen was unearthed as an unlikely rugby tour venue for 1959. The name Penguin RFC was adopted and we set off. Thirty-eight years later those same two players are still at the helm. Mason, chairman, and Wright, secretary, guiding the club through the first year of rugby professionalism.

In 1959, rugby in Denmark and Sweden was in the beginners stage. The game in Denmark had been founded and kept going by a remarkable man called Eigil Lund – a mounted policeman in Copenhagen. His love of rugby and his dedication to the game under extensive financial difficulties would be a beacon of light in the present-day climate of money and greed.

Tony and Mike Mason. The first father and son combination to play at Twickenham.

Rugby was so backward in Denmark in 1959 that the tour became an instructional and missionary one. After each game we picked two teams, mixing Danish players with Penguins, and coached the Danes as they played. This was to be the role of the Penguins for the next 38 years – as coaches and ambassadors. The motto, *On court le ballon à la main* (They run with the ball in the hand), was adopted.

For the next 38 years we were to tour the world, spreading and promoting the great game of rugby wherever we could. During those years all the players and officials paid their own way – and that is how it remained during 37 years of amateurism. The late Gwynne Walters, the great Welsh referee, described us as the last of the truly amateur corinthians. The club has no subscription and has relied entirely on voluntary donations from its very generous honorary vice-presidents to cover the cost of equipment and touring expenses.

In 1967, we had a lucky break where, as a result of a chance meeting, we were invited to supply the opposition team to play at the RFU headquarters – at Twickenham. This match had a profound effect on the future of the club as we were able to put out a team containing 10 Lions and other internationals, including the likes of Ron Jacobs,

Tony Horton, Bill Paterson, Andy Hancock and Mike Davies. We made history with our co-founder Alan Wright playing in the back row and our other founder Tony Mason at full back with his son Mike at fly half – the first time a father and son had played at Twickenham.

In 1968, the late Robin Prescott, then the secretary of the RFU, asked the club to help by taking a tour to Belgium and Gambia as both countries had a gripe with the RFU. This we did willingly. Two very successful tours were undertaken and our place on the touring circuit was established. Tours were made in 1970 to California, in 1972 to Gambia again, in 1973 to Rhodesia and South Africa and in 1974 we paid our first visit to Bermuda.

This was a golden era for the Penguins as we were able to take famous players to all these countries and our tours had gained the reputation amongst the players as something special.

After our South Africa tour in 1974 we were given an open invitation to return. The *Cape Times* carried the headline, 'Danie Craven said the Penguins are welcome to play here anytime whilst they play rugby like this,' after our game at Newlands – even though we lost! We had included Lions, Fergus Slattery, Chris Rea and Bill Steele and internationals Dave Watt, Wally McMaster, Tony Ensor, Ian Robertson, Nairn MacEwan and Alex Finlayson.

We put Bermuda on the map with our first tour and it rapidly became the first-choice touring destination. We toured on a four-yearly basis until we were pushed out by the Bermuda Classic.

The Penguins pictured after their final game against Russia which made them winners of the tournament celebrating the 60th anniversary of the Russian Revolution.

In 1977, the RFU asked the Penguins to represent them as England were unable to send a team to play in a tournament in Russia being held to celebrate the 60th anniversary of the Russian Revolution. We were able to pick a squad containing a mix of 14 Lions and other international players and beat Czechoslovakia, Poland, Romania and Russia One and Two to win the tournament unbeaten.

In 1979, we celebrated the centenary of the Sri Lanka RU followed by a tour to Argentina in 1980. In 1982 and 1986 we toured Bermuda and to celebrate our Silver Jubilee had a marvellous tour to Brazil in 1984, where they nearly killed us with kindness.

Martin Offiah holds the Penguins mascot as the side are introduced to the crowd at the 1988 Hong Kong 7s.

In 1987 we received an urgent phone call from the chairman of the Hong Kong 7s Committee inviting us to send a team to the 7s as they had had a late withdrawal. Though we only had 12 days to select a squad and arrive in Hong Kong we accepted without hesitation. Fortunately a young unknown Martin Offiah had played for us against Oxford University earlier in the season and was available. He proved a sensation and we had a very successful tournament beating the French Barbarians, the previous years' finalists, in the first round, eventually losing to the All Blacks in the semi-finals.

The next year we were again beaten by the All Blacks in the semi-finals, but our squad was much stronger containing David Kirk, World Cup-winning All Black captain, Wayne Smith, winning All Black captain at a previous Hong Kong 7s, Bill Calcraft who had captained Australia, David Pickering, captain of Wales, Rob Wainwright who went on to become captain of Scotland, and John Bentley, who became a famous Lion in 1997.

In 1990 we won the Calcutta Cup in Calcutta, a cup presented by British Airways to celebrate 100 years of rugby in Calcutta, and we went on to win the Italian 7s in Sicily in 1993 and 1994.

The RFU recommended the Penguins to the Malaysia RU in 1993 and we won the Malaysian International 10s Tournament in Kuala Lumpur at our first attempt and again in 1994. In August 1994 we had the unique distinction of winning the Stockholm 10s on Sunday 21 August, defeating Sweden at the 15-a-side game the following Tuesday, and then beating the Penguin Club (named after us because they liked the way we played rugby) on Sunday 28 August in Copenhagen to win the Nordic 7s. Winners at 7s, 10s, and 15s, in the space of a week.

Brian Moore wrote in his autobiography, 'The Penguins are widely known as the poor man's Barbarians, but for me they have always been preferable because they have some of the status and the glamour of the Barbarians, but none of the bullshit. Their officials … put together a well-balanced mixture [of players]. There would be a few caps who had not become fixtures in their national teams, a few experienced players nearing retirement and some promising players. I have always held a soft spot for the Penguins.'

Our selection policy has been successful, enabling us to play carefree rugby for enjoyment, to entertain our hosts and usually to win. The players have played their part in playing attractive rugby and being ambassadors both on and off the field – so much so that we have always been invited to return and have played in Copenhagen five times, Malaysia five times, Bermuda four times, Hong Kong three times, Sicily three times, and Belgium three times, *inter alia*.

The 1996–97 season was the first of the new professional game, and with it came problems. The only games we play in England are against Oxford and Cambridge Universities usually in February and March and this season there was an understandable reluctance to release players, partly due to congestion and uncertainty with fixtures.

The more enlightened of the coaches realised that clubs like the Penguins could be useful to the professional clubs with overlapping squads where they are unable to keep their players match-fit. By allowing them to play for the Penguins they could keep them happy and ready for action. We hope we can continue to help the clubs without interfering with their team preparations.

In March 1997 we obtained very generous sponsorship through the Hongkong and Shanghai Bank and this enabled us to carry out a tour to Prague and Budapest in June. We have now played in 34 countries against teams of 51 nationalities, and nearly 100 players have played for the Penguins before representing their countries.

Derek Wyatt wrote in the *1994 International Rugby Almanack*, under the heading 'Ninety-Six Clubs plus Four Unusual Sides': 'If there was a vote by players the world over for the most popular club, the result would be the Penguins RFC. The odd thing about this lot is, except for very rare occasions and usually for charity, they only play outside the UK. As a consequence few readers will have heard of them.

'Formed over 30 years ago by Tony Mason and Alan Wright, they have trod where very few rugby clubs, provincial sides or even international XVs have wanted to go.

'Tony Mason has an uncanny knack, some call it talent, of selecting players from around the world before their own national selectors were aware of their abilities – Maurice Colclough and Ollie Campbell to USSR in 1977, Stuart Evans to Brazil in 1984, Andy Nicol to Calcutta 1990, Eric Peters to Kuala Lumpur 1993, *inter alia*.

'The Penguins really ought to be adopted by the Lord's Taverners as their worldwide ambassadors, and Twickenham should reward them by giving them the last fixture of all incoming tours. They have done much more than the Barbarians have or ever will do for the game.'

We hope we will be allowed to continue to promote the game.

Midland Bank congratulates Martin Johnson, captain of the 1997 British Lions

Midland Bank

Member HSBC *Group*

Issued by Midland Bank plc

THE BRITISH LIONS
IN SOUTH AFRICA

AGAINST ALL ODDS

BY **MICK CLEARY**

It was an easy bet to strike. The Springboks had only ever been beaten twice at home in a series in over a century of official competition. Willie John McBride's band of brawling brothers had taken on the South Africans at their own abrasive game back in 1974 and come away decisive winners. It was another 22 years before any other side managed to get the better of them over a series, albeit aided by apartheid isolation for many of those years. However, it took several generations of mighty All Blacks before the South African colours were finally lowered in 1996, Sean Fitzpatrick's side winning the series 2–1. And that was that. So many other teams down through the decades had come with hopes high of wrestling the initiative away from the Bokke. None of them succeeded. South Africa had always been a hard, stark, unforgiving place, wonderful to view, great to tour, but inhospitable if your colour or politics did not fit. Rugby was the totem of the Afrikaner, a reflection of his virility and his impenetrability. The line was defended at all costs.

Martin Johnson's 1997 Lions did not even travel with high hopes. The Springboks had carried all before them on their winter tour to the northern hemisphere, comprehensively outplaying Wales in the final match. That day they played with dash, cunning and dynamic pace, proving too fast and too powerful in the middle five even for a Welsh team playing to the best of their own form. On top of all this many of the British and Irish players had to crawl to the finishing tape of the longest and most attritional domestic season in the history of the game. Many were suffering from chronic strains and injuries, including the captain Martin Johnson, who would have had an operation on a troublesome groin in normal circumstances.

The Five Nations championship had not yielded too many nuggets of optimism either. England had demolished the Celtic challenge with disdain, running up record scores against Scotland, Wales and Ireland. England had then faltered against France suggesting that their own sense of themselves was not as truly assured as it appeared when tackling physically weaker opponents. The prognosis, then, was simple – the Lions would be flattened and would do well to avoid being humiliated. Springboks Joel Stransky and François Pienaar, both playing the latter part of the season in England, predicted a 3–0 triumph for the Springboks. It was logic rather than bias which prompted such claims.

It's as well to recall these perspectives when assessing the 1997 Lions. They were virtual no-hopers when they first met up at the Oatlands Hotel just outside Weybridge in Surrey. There were not too many quibbles about the 35-man squad selected, nor were there any qualms about the management team in place. Fran Cotton as manager and coaches Ian McGeechan and Jim Telfer had been round the rugby block many times and had, for the most part, come away with considerable credit. No, everything that could have been done had been done. But still the gloom-mongers spun their tales of woe. It was hard to unearth a dissenting voice. Not one person I came across fancied the Lions. The most favourable return was that they might nick one of the Tests, in all probability the first in Cape Town before the Springboks got into their stride.

We'd been lured towards our damning verdicts by some very persuasive evidence. There were the tales of woe of every touring team down the years, the ragged and worn physical state of most of the players, the ritzy PR profile of the southern hemisphere's Super 12 competition – a template of infallibility for rugby everywhere, or so they would have us believe – and, finally, there was the murderous schedule the Lions had undertaken. In the run-up to Cape Town the Lions were to play Northern Transvaal, Gauteng (Transvaal) and Natal within the space of eight days, mini-Test matches in themselves. All in all, the Lions' chances did not amount to a hill of beans.

Oh, we of little faith. We'd been down this track with Ian McGeechan before. In 1989 no one fancied the Lions after the first Test. But back they came under McGeechan's tutelage to take the series against Australia. Again in 1993 the intimidating spectre of All Blacks dominance haunted every attempt at an optimistic forecast. The Lions, though, were within a very dubious refereeing decision of winning the first Test, the penalty being awarded against rather than in favour of Dean Richards, Grant Fox then doing the business for New Zealand from 40 metres. The Lions put in a Herculean effort to take the second Test. The All Blacks dug very deep into their psyche to hit back in the deciding Test. That party, although competitive and powerful in the Tests, finished woefully in the mid-week games. There was a sharp divide in talent and application between the Test team and the dirt-trackers; so sharp that some of the boys might well have been on different tours. The collapse was dramatic and shameful, the last two games being conceded with scarcely a whimper. If anything those dispiriting defeats to Waikato, and Hawke's Bay in particular, hardened the approach of this tour party. The management were determined that there would be no repetition of the New Zealand fiasco – no draining of morale by poor commitment in midweek games, no abusing of the Lions' badge by inadequate performances.

That was the singular aim of the 1997 squad. But how to implement it? Words are easy – deeds are another thing altogether. It would help if the whole squad could be on their competitive toes, all battling for a Test place right to the very last week. That is exactly what did happen – a state of affairs which the management admitted was beyond even their wildest hopes. It was no fluke, though, and they should credit themselves for bringing it off. The key to any successful team, at whatever level and in whatever sport, is selection. If you haven't got the right players, ones with talent, dedication, nerve and heart, then no amount of good coaching and fine planning will be of any real use. With a Lions party it's not just a matter of picking the obvious players either, those who have been dominant for their country beating up the less accomplished nations of that particular championship. In latter years England has been top dog, far and away the most consistent and the most physically imperious of all the home countries. Their pack in particular has called all the shots throughout the 1990s – stronger, bigger and more influential than any of the Celts. And yet the original selection for the first Test contained four Irishmen – Paul Wallace, Keith Wood, Jeremy Davidson and Eric Miller (who withdrew with 'flu) – and one unheralded Scot, Tom Smith. The vaunted English front five was blown away in the selection rooms.

The four Irishmen who made such an impact on the tour take a stroll down the Durban beach – (from left to right) Keith Wood, Jeremy Davidson, Paul Wallace and Eric Miller.

McGeechan and Co. had picked players not just with form but with potential. They had also chosen players who would fit neatly into the preferred game plan, one which had been hatched not in the pre-tour get-together in Surrey but nine months earlier down in South Africa itself. No sooner had McGeechan been appointed than he headed off to South Africa to watch the All Blacks take on the Boks in a three-match series. This was to be the first fully professional tour and the management were determined to approach it in a professional manner. In the days of old, players had to count the seconds on once-a-week phone calls home as they watched their daily pittance of an allowance drain away. The press corps would invariably adopt a player and try to look after them for surreptitious calls on the office phone or subsidise their drinking on expense accounts. As recently as 1993, the players were reliant on the tour kitty to fund any extras.

McGeechan put in his request and it was approved immediately. The Home Unions committee showed themselves to be enlightened and progressive, and it's not very often that phrase has been written. But credit where it is due. They embarked on this tour in the same steel-eyed, detailed and committed manner as anyone else in the party. The backing the management received from the likes of Bob Weighill, secretary of the Home Unions, Ray Williams, chairman, and John Lawrence, treasurer, was first-rate.

McGeechan headed south to watch and to learn. It was a journey of discovery, by far the most important two weeks of any Lions pre-planning ever undertaken. 'I saw how the All Blacks beat the Springboks and therefore saw how we would beat them too,' said McGeechan.

Gregor Townsend and Lawrence Dallaglio implement the Lions' defensive strategy – it proved such a success that South Africa's fly half Henry Honiball was dropped for the third Test.

The All Blacks played fast and wide, stretching the South Africans who were much more at ease and effective in traditional channels of play. Their middle five – back row and half backs – was the axis through which they worked most of their plays. Nullify that threat and a lot of the Springbok potency was diminished. South Africa worked a lot off Honiball at fly half – a big, bruising player who would attack the gain line himself only to push the ball either inside to Teichmann or to one of the other back row, or flip it on to Mulder or le Roux at his shoulder. McGeechan made his notes and plotted his strategy. The Lions would attack South Africa at their strongest point. They would target Honiball. The Lions fly half, whoever that might be, would push hard and fast at Honiball while two others, scrum half and flanker, would immediately fill the gaps where

Honiball might expect to find his support. Instead, all he would find was a red British Lions shirt. The result was that Honiball had to stand deeper and deeper to find space. He never did find it and was dropped for the third Test – a compliment to McGeechan's plan and the players' execution of it. The South Africans never did figure out what was happening to them, that the squeeze was deliberately being put on them. They simply wondered aloud as to what the hell Honiball was doing, going back into the pocket to make the plays.

It's strange that in the age of video analysis they couldn't unravel the mystery. So much of international rugby these days is carefully choreographed. That is not to say that the players are locked into robotic programmes where there is to be no deviation from the pre-ordained norm. In the hands of a poor coach that will be the case. In the hands of a good coach the use of video tapes and monitored sequences of play is a liberating force. Harlequins coach, Andy Keast, spent hours and hours locked away in various hotel rooms around South Africa scrutinising video tapes of the Lions themselves and the opposition. From that he used a specially commissioned computer to isolate the contribution of particular players and particular aspects of their play. Every week on tour, each Lions' player received video highlights, often no more than five to ten minutes long, of their own play.

The video tapes also allowed McGeechan to impress on the players how the chosen method of attack would actually work. In watching the All Blacks, McGeechan had noticed how vulnerable the 'Boks were if taken out of their designated defensive channels. It was not enough merely to spin the ball wide for the drift defence could easily cope with that. Instead, the Lions were to slipstream the ball-carrier, trailing his run and then hitting an angle late but fast. They would actually come off-line, a complete contradiction to the standard coaching manual which advocates running straight. It was a mix of the French at their best and Aussie Rugby League sides at their most dynamic. It sounds easy in theory, but it took McGeechan nine months of planning and several intense weeks of training to put it into practice.

For Ian McGeechan, decision-makers such as Gregor Townsend held the key necessary to unlock the South African defence.

That was the playing philosophy – to play with the ball in hand from all parts of the field, to be aggressive in defence and to attack South Africa at their supposedly strongest link. The selection reflected the strategy. There was an emphasis on decision-makers, players who would not be afraid to tilt the run of play one way or the other. Far from being programmed to run only to designated parts of the field McGeechan wanted players who could sniff the wind, sense where the openings were and take the play to those parts. Gregor Townsend was groomed as the Test fly half – a player who might have frailties when it came to controlled kicking, but whose creative instincts would help unlock the tightest of defences. There was to be a strong Rugby League contingent – Scott Gibbs, Allan Bateman, John Bentley, Alan Tait, Scott Quinnell and David Young – guys used to playing at an intense level and constantly in the face of the opposition.

McGeechan picked up other useful tips from the All Blacks. They recommended a 35-man squad so as to give the specialist positions such as hooker and scrum half a rest from bench duties. The All Blacks had also brought all their own training gear with them, from tackle bags to scrum-machines. It didn't just ease the logistics of the tour, it also gave them a feeling of self-containment and control. The mood of a touring party, right down to the smallest facet, is crucial.

Fran Cotton had been busy too. He recognised the importance of planning. He visited every hotel and training venue during a 12-day trip, making sure that facilities, medical back-up, and the right food would all be in place. He asked for, and got, the biggest back-up staff ever on a Lions tour: from doctor, James Robson, to kicking coach, Dave Alred, to administrative secretary, Samantha 'Lioness' Peters. There were 12 of them in all and every one of them carried their weight. The Lions squad felt and looked professional – the players merely carried on in that vein.

Finally, Cotton arranged for a specialist group, Impact, to run the pre-tour camp at Weybridge. The company specialised in team-building in industry, encouraging groups to cooperate more readily and efficiently. And so the first few days in the wooded surrounds of the Oatlands Hotel were spent far from any rugby balls. There was bridge-building, rescue operations across no man's land, beer-crate stacking, canoe exercises, all designed to create team spirit.

'We wanted something that was fun but with a purpose, too,' said McGeechan. Many of the relationships which showed up so well over the next eight weeks sprung from those early days.

And so to South Africa. The Lions had the plan and they had the players. Had they got the will, the courage and the conviction to succeed? It was rarely in doubt. From the very first minutes of the opening game against an Eastern Province XV it was obvious that the Lions were on a special mission. On a hot Port Elizabeth afternoon they took the game to the opposition with a sense of style and purpose, as if, in truth, they had been playing together for a couple of years not a couple of weeks. Guscott had pranced over the line within nine minutes with all the ease and grace of the star performer he is. It was the build-up though which would have alarmed Springbok observers – sustained, varied and assured. Unfortunately for the Springboks there weren't many observers there. Or at subsequent games. Or if there were, they were looking in the wrong place for the wrong things.

So much of the early comment was focused on the Lions' apparent soft underbelly in the forwards. The Lions were dubbed 'pussycats'. It's true that there were difficulties in the scrum, but these were no more than teething problems, a lack of familiarisation. The key to any scrummage is timing. The forwards had spent little time together. Nor, too, were they used to the massive hit-and-shove style of South African scrummaging. In the northern hemisphere front rows have to crouch, touch, pause and engage. The South Africans felt confident, particularly when the Lions lost their fifth game of the tour 35–30 to Northern Transvaal. The Lions made a woeful start in that match, their worst half hour on tour, and were exposed in the tight scrum itself.

It was seen as the Lions first big test and they had failed it. But again the South Africans went for the obvious, simplistic interpretation. It was almost as if they were afraid to contemplate a disturbing truth – that in their previous games the Lions had looked very dangerous and were playing a type of game no one locally would have associated with the northern hemisphere. Eastern Province were beaten 39–11, Border eventually overcome in a rain-lashed mudbath 18–14, before the Lions really found their gears. Western Province were impressively seen off in Cape Town, 38–21 and the supposed might of Mpumalanga, newcomers to the top rankings, dismantled 64–14. That match saw the brutal stamping of Doddie Weir by Marius Bosman. Weir's cruciate ligament was damaged and he was off the tour. Bosman should have been suspended for at least a year. Instead he was fined £1,250 – it was an insult to the game.

In all these matches the Lions played with ambition, perception and clinical finishing power. They were launching attacks from all parts of the field, unperturbed by any local difficulties in the scrummage. It's true that they wobbled that afternoon in Pretoria, but the Springboks did themselves no favours by latching on to the one area of weakness, one moreover which is more easily rectified than any other phase of the game. There is always a direct return on flesh bruised on a scrummaging machine. The Lions had just the man to bruise some flesh for the good of the cause.

Jim Telfer was the forwards coach, a man feared throughout the rugby land for the severity of his tongue. The truth is more complex. Telfer delights in hiding his wry wit, natural charm and softness, behind a stern mask. What he does, he does for the good of the team not simply for effect. He has a massive knowledge of forward play round the world and keeps in sprightly step with the times. The Lions' forwards always respected him – some grew to love him for they appreciated his care, his wisdom and his understanding.

The midweek game against Gauteng in Ellis Park, Johannesburg, was a defining moment. The opposition was good, the venue intimidating. Two defeats in succession would have seen the tour momentum come to a grinding halt. It didn't. As happened throughout the tour the mid-week side were magnificent. John Bentley scored a wonder try and the entire side defended with real edge. Gauteng were beaten 20–14 and the whole squad celebrated. They were all in this together. Three days later we saw exciting evidence as Currie Cup champions Natal were seen off 42–12. Bring on the Springboks.

It is customary for touring teams to field a shadow XV the week before the Test. All the combinations are usually settled by this time and it is vital that they have at least one full match together. These Lions were different. The push for places was fierce. There was nothing else for it but to give everyone a fair crack. It meant that the tour spirit stayed keen and healthy. McGeechan admits that he would happily have taken the field with at least five different selections from the Test team eventually selected. The calibre of the squad was that good. Bateman, Leonard, Shaw, Rodber (originally, although Miller withdrew), Williams or Regan at hooker, Back, Tony Underwood and even Mike Catt, a late arrival on tour for the injured Paul Grayson, could consider themselves unlucky.

The first Test in Cape Town was a memorable day. The play was intense, the atmosphere, with 5,000 British and Irish in town, electric. Once again the Lions' defence was awesome. McGeechan had preached the need to be patient, to absorb pressure because their time would come and the Springboks would not be able to cope. And it happened just that way. Jenkins kicked his goals, five in all to keep the Lions in contention at 16–15 midway through the second half, du Randt and Bennett having scored tries for South Africa. Then the Lions struck, with Matt Dawson scoring an outrageous opportunistic try seven minutes from time. Dawson broke from a scrum on the Springbok 22, shaped to pass, checked, dummied again and the entire South African nation looked infield. Dawson, meanwhile, headed to the tryline. Alan Tait wrapped up the 25–16 victory on full-time with a well-worked try. The forwards, particularly the props, Smith and Wallace, came of age.

The icing on the cake, as Alan Tait touches down in the final moments of the victorious first Test.

No side which had won a first Test in South Africa had ever then lost a series. The weight of history hung heavy over the Springboks. They would be fighting for their lives at King's Park, Durban, the following Saturday. They played as if they were, too. The opening 20 minutes was the most ferocious I've ever seen in Test rugby. The Boks ripped into the Lions, but once more the Lions rode the stormy seas and then launched their own retaliatory missile – the right boot of Neil Jenkins. The closest the Lions got to the Springbok half was a penalty two metres from half way. Jenkins kicked it. The Lions had absolutely nothing of the game yet led 3–0.

This Test was won on character and belief. It was not a lucky victory, but it was an improbable one. South Africa had all the play, all the possession and all the positions yet they could not shake off the Lions. The Lions had spent hours in training on their defensive patterns also honing their self-discipline in the process. They gave away only one penalty in the entire second half, a phenomenal return. South Africa scored three tries through van der Westhuizen, Montgomery and Joubert. The Lions scored five penalties through Jenkins, the last bringing the scores level at 15–15 with six minutes remaining. The Lions heads were higher at this point. They hacked downfield, won the line out, drove, Townsend darted but was checked, the ball was recylced, Guscott's sweet boot was swinging and suddenly the whole place was rocking. It was a tumultuous scene of celebration, a canvas of British and Irish flags waving across a sultry Durban nightscape.

The final Test was a peak too far. Ironically the Lions played their best rugby of the series in going down 35–16. What they lacked was the focus and concentration of the previous two weeks. They made more mistakes than before and gave away more penalties. But given that they lost five players that week to injury and illness and one more, Tim Rodber, on the morning of the match, it was a rousing display. When Matt Dawson closed the scores to 23–16 with 15 minutes remaining you sensed that the Springboks were about to cave in. But they were hell bent on avoiding a first-ever series whitewash. They finished strongly with the Lions simply having nothing left in the tank. Snyman and Rossouw scored two tries for South Africa in the last six minutes.

The Lions did a lap of honour around Ellis Park. They richly deserved it. For spirit and conviction they have had few equals in Lions' history. They played superb rugby in the provincial matches, the 52–30 win over Free State between the first and second Tests being the highlight. They will be remembered for their positive outlook, their dedication to the cause and the wonderful warmth of their squad spirit. Every last man was a hero in his own right.

Lions' captain Martin Johnson holds aloft the trophy – only the third captain in Test history to lead his side to a series victory in South Africa.

You're looking into the future...

AUTO FOCUS f=5mm 1:2.8/5.6/11

MAIN SW
• CAMERA
• PLAY

MODE
SET

LCD DIGITAL CAMERA

SANYO

digiCAM

THE NEW DIGITAL STILL CAMERA FROM

SANYO

THE BEST OF A BAD JOB

BY **JOHN REASON**

Now that South Africa is back in the Commonwealth, the four Home Unions should recommend Carel du Plessis and Gary Teichmann for knighthoods. Indeed they must, because no one has done more for the cause of British and Irish rugby in the last 20 years than the 1997 coach of the Springboks and his captain. And what makes the whole of this imperative and so much more attractive is that both du Plessis and Teichmann are such thoroughly nice fellows.

They certainly did not spare themselves in their efforts to be the most obliging and accommodating of hosts for the 1997 British Lions tour of South Africa. They strewed that lovely country with flowers and in the first two of the three Tests they even gave the Lions Springboks to eat. This presented the Lions with the series and spared them any sleepless nights in the last week of the tour. Greater love hath no man. For make no

Even though the Lions had a genuine fly half in Neil Jenkins, he was forced to play out of position – at full back.

mistake, those British and Irish Lions needed every scrap of that charity because rugby in the four Home Unions is now at a very low ebb – and that is putting it kindly.

When they set off for the tour, the Lions did not have a front row. They did not have a fly half, and they did not have a full back. When they finished the tour, they were in exactly the same plight. No team has ever survived a Test series in South Africa with deficiencies as profound as that. The spine of the team, that vital backbone, was and remained three parts jelly.

What was even more extraordinary was that the Lions *did* have a thoroughly competent fly half in every facet of the game – by the name of Neil Jenkins. They chose not to play him in that position, however, except when a mid-match injury in the key game against Transvaal forced them to move him infield.

All it needed was a straightforward fly-half hob, and of course, Jenkins fitted the role perfectly. The game he played that evening was comfortably the best fly-half performance of the tour, and he capped it with the greatest pressure conversion kicked on tour. That kick to convert Austin Healey's second-half try gave the Lions the lead and it gave them the impetus and the confidence to go on and win the match. Jenkins' remarkable goal-kicking won the series.

For the rest of the tour, Jenkins had to play full back to accommodate the dogma emanating from the Lions' coach Ian McGeechan that Gregor Townsend had to play fly half. Townsend is a back with remarkable pace and footwork, and considerable

powers of penetration. He is well suited to play outside centre or wing, but he is not a fly half. He is not what might be called a 'professional' in that position, in the way that Jenkins is. Townsend does not kick well enough. He has not acquired the positional experience to be a strategist. By sticking to him as they did, the Lions selectors lumbered him with the impossible burden of thinking he had to pull a rabbit out of the hat almost every time he was given the ball.

He was never allowed to lull the opposition. To have spells in which he just did bread and butter things quietly and competently. He was never allowed to be a comfortable and unremarkable part of the landscape. Instead, he had to be Vesuvius, constantly in a state of erruption. That presented South Africa with no problems. They just put three men on him.

Even when Townsend was injured and not available for the third Test, the Lions still did not choose Jenkins at fly half. They chose Mike Catt instead, who had been flown in as a replacement for the injured Paul Grayson. But the game Catt played at Ellis Park was the worst I have ever seen played by a Lions fly half. He did everything wrong.

So Jenkins remained stuck at full back, as he had been all through, even though he is doubtful under the high ball and even less assured when he has to turn and chase those raking, wide diagonal kicks. But the strange thing was – and the longer the tour lasted, the more unbelieveable it became – South Africa did not attack Jenkins as a full back. They did not bomb him with high kicks. They gave him one or two, which made him look uncomfortable, but they never flattened him. They never turned him and stretched him wide. Even Jenkins was surprised. Early in the tour, when the Lions beat a quite dreadful Natal non-team in Durban, he raised his eyebrows publicly afterwards by saying that he could not understand why Natal had not bombed him. 'But,' said he, with doubtful wisdom, 'I dare say I will get a few in the first Test next week.'

At that point, some of us took a deep, deep breath. Soft targets should not make such admissions. But incredible as it is to relate, the bombers did not take off in the Test in Cape Town, and they stayed grounded for most of the tour.

South Africa did not help themselves either by removing all their Test squad players from the provincial games against the Lions. This demeaned the tour. It was an insult to the Lions. But it did far, far more damage to the Springboks, because there is no quicker way to learn the strengths and weaknesses of opponents than by playing against them.

To be fair, the Lions could do nothing about their front row. They took five props on tour, and not one of them was anywhere near the requisite standard. The Border front row thrashed them in the second game, and when Gary Pagel demolished Jason Leonard in the third match against Western Province, the Lions must have thought their number was up. They knew that Pagel could not even get into the Springbok squad, never mind the Test team. Os du Randt was the blockbuster in front of him.

So all the Lions could do was make the best of a bad job. This entailed their tight head dropping his right shoulder and boring in on the opposing hooker so that if the pressure became too great, the scrum simply collapsed.

After four of those scrums, of course, the tight head in question should have been penalised four times and sent off the field. And after four more scrums, the replacement tight head would also have been penalised four times, and he also would have been sent off. So after about half an hour, the referee would have had to abandon the match because the International Board, in their infinite lack of wisdom, have decreed that if a team does not have a specialist front-row forward as a replacement, the match must stop.

Whether they are aware of it or not, this assured destruction scenario must be in the back of the minds of all international referees. So if, in the early part of the match, they penalise a tight head twice for collapsing a scrum, they are more than reluctant to do it again. Jim Telfer, the Lions' forward coach, probably gambled on this and won all his bets.

I watched one of the Tests in the company of two ex-international referees, both South African, who were justifiably shouting 'penalty' or 'penalty try' every time the scrum went down, but clearly neither had thought the matter through to the consequences of penalising repeated infringement. I suspect that Jim Telfer had.

Even so, the South African front row should have been able to deal with the problem, particularly as du Randt is so big and so hugely strong. But the further the tour went, the more it became apparent that for all their country's great tradition of scrummaging, South Africa are still technically as naive as they were when the British and Irish Lions demolished them in 1974.

Now *that* Lions team could scrummage. So much so that Hannes Marais, an erstwhile Springbok captain, got in more than enough flying hours to qualify for a pilot's licence. That Lions team frequently kicked the ball out of the scrum deliberately, just to prolong the awful suffering of their opponents. And that Lions team had only four props, not five. And they played twice as many games.

Du Randt, properly coached, should have been capable of destroying the Lions' scrum. Instead, he spent most of his time playing moonies to the left field – he was turned so far inwards that he showed nothing but his backside to the touch judge and the crowd. This also killed the lock scrummaging behind him.

So instead of sapping the strength of the Lions, South Africa found themselves beaten for fitness in the first Test and were dumbfounded when the Lions scored two tries in the last quarter to steal the match.

The one scored by Matt Dawson will go into Lions' Test history. He had gone into the Lions' Test team as the replacement for the injured Rob Howley, who was a scrum half the Springboks feared. They knew Howley was a key player. So when Howley had to leave the tour, they relaxed. Dawson? Who was he? A so-so player. Lucky to be there.

Matt Dawson outwits the South African defence to score the crucial try in the first Test at Cape Town.

Only in the team because he played for the club Ian McGeechan coached. That thinking proved to be very costly.

With ten minutes left, the Lions forced an attacking scrum. As the ball came out, Dawson saw a lot of space on the blind side. Unconsidered he may have been, but slow on the uptake he most definitely was not. He went through the gap like a ferret and drifted out to the right. At that moment, Ieuan Evans came in off the right wing and hit the after burners. If Howley had been carrying the ball, the Springboks would have ignored Evans. They knew what damage Howley could do and they would have drilled him into the back row of the stand. But Dawson? No track record. So, fleetingly, the cover defence checked when Dawson dummied to lob a one-handed pass back inside. No fewer than five defenders hesitated.

Then, with a nonchalance that was supreme, Dawson pulled the ball back, just as if he was Jeeves deciding that this was not exactly the right moment to decant the *Château Petrus*, and kept going for the corner. And why not? There was no one in the way. Not a soul. It was priceless. It also won the Test.

As if that was not enough, Teichmann threw away the second Test in Durban with five of the most extraordinary decisions I have ever seen on a rugby field. The Springboks had six kicks at goal, any two of which would have won them the match and the series, but they missed them all because Teichmann gave five of the six kicks to the wrong kicker.

He had two left-footed kickers in Percy Montgomery and André Joubert and one right-footed kicker in Henry Honiball. Montgomery had been brought in to strengthen the goal kicking, and the first two kicks early in the game would have suited him perfectly because they were just to the right of the posts. Instead, Teichmann gave them to Honiball and he missed them both.

The first was a poor kick, but the second was well struck, so when South Africa were given a third kick, just to the left of the posts, it would have been a formality for Honiball. Instead, the kick was given to Montgomery who, winning his first cap, and kicking from the wrong side of the posts, looked as if he was shaking at the knees. He lost balance and missed. Easily.

The Springboks had three kicks at goal in the second half, too. One of those to the right of the posts was given to Montgomery, but his confidence had been destroyed. The other two were both wrongly allocated. Near the end, when Joubert brushed aside John Bentley to score in the left corner, the only kicker who could have converted the try was Honiball. Instead, Teichmann gave the kick to Joubert whose kick went nowhere near.

So a dropped goal by the silky Jeremy Guscott at the end was enough to win the match and the series for the Lions. Never did a team have more cause to be grateful to their opponents.

The Lions' problems were aggravated by an avalanche of injuries. They lost 11 players in the first 12 games, and simply could not have fielded a team if they had been required to play another match after the final Test. But what the Lions did have, and thanks to du Plessis and Teichmann it was enough to keep them in business, was a defence, a goal-kicker and a line out.

The defence was manufactured by the ex-Rugby League players in the team, and I have never seen or heard anything like it. They attacked every opposing ball carrier with three men. One head on, and the other two ready to pincer. This offensive defence originated in American football, but to be sustained through multiple phases of attack on a rugby field, depended on communication between the players for its success. The noise was deafening – everyone shouting to warn of gaps which had to be filled.

(Above) Jeremy Guscott unleashes his right boot to score the dropped goal that secured the series for the Lions.

Scott Gibbs on the offensive, but it was in defence that he caused the most damage to the Springboks.

The defence pivoted around Scott Gibbs in the Lions centre. He was immense. Comfortably the man of the series. Yet he might not have played in the Tests if Allan Bateman had been fit because it looked as if McGeechan's original idea was to play Bateman and Guscott outside Townsend.

What Gibbs did in the first Test was extraordinary. What the Springboks did was even more extraordinary. Wave after wave of their midfield players ran at Gibbs, and every time he smashed them down. Yet even though they went off the field for ten minutes at half time, and had the chance to ask their coach if, 'Please sir, could we run at someone else, because Mr Gibbs keeps on hurting us?', they never changed their target. They never attacked the far less abrasive Guscott or sought to inconvenience Jenkins.

Jeremy Davidson was a key line-out player too, because Martin Johnson, the Lions captain, had been so played into the ground by his club that he was carrying a groin injury and was only a shadow of his real self. It was a bad tour for most of England's forwards.

Predictably, with the series won and lost, the third Test was a disaster for the Lions. The team they chose made no sense, and the way they tried to play made even less sense. They chose Jenkins at full back instead of fly half. They chose Guscott at centre instead of Bateman. They chose Underwood on the wing instead of Guscott. And horror upon horror, particulary after what had happened at Welkom the previous Tuesday, they chose Catt at fly half.

The Lions also chose Mark Regan at hooker instead of Barry Williams and they chose Rob Wainwright on the flank instead of keeping Lawrence Dallaglio there and bringing in a ball handler and ball winner as capable as Tony Diprose at No.8. They also chose Neil Back instead of Richard Hill. All of this diminished the Lions' prospects.

The way the Lions played that last Test diminished those chances even more. Even the All Blacks have found it impossible to win the last match of a South African tour at Ellis Park, but instead of sticking to reality and grinding it out, the Lions went out to play as if they were the 1971 Lions, and they did not have nearly enough strike runners to do that.

Matt Dawson dives over the line to keep the Lions faint hopes of a series whitewash alive.

They tried to keep the line-out throw by copying the Andy Haden strategy that beat the 1993 Lions in New Zealand. They put an embargo on kicking for touch, but they did not have a tactical kicker anywhere near the class of Grant Fox, so they rarely pressurised the Springbok under the ball. Not only that, the Lions chose not to use any other form of kicking. They just tried to retain possession of the ball and although they occasionally succeeded for minutes on end, they hardly ever advanced.

This suited the Springboks. 'Right,' they said. 'If you are not going to kick, all we have to do is block up the middle.' Which they did.

There were very few high kicks and no attempt to find space with them, even though when the ball hit the ground it caused problems for both defences. So the Lions lost composure. They lost turnovers. They were 13 points down in ten minutes. And their fly half was sentencing his centres to death by running sideways. The Lions also bought yet another dummy from a glory-lover as obvious and as predictable as Joost van der Westhuizen. A dummy is all he has to sell.

Only the meticulous precision of Jenkins' goal-kicking and another close range try by Dawson kept the Lions' faint hopes alive for an hour. But that was only a gesture, and as sure as night follows day, a modestly endowed Springbok team swept in for two tries in the last few minutes, running easily past a defence which had given its all in the earlier battles, and could give no more.

Time to celebrate for the Lions after securing an improbable 2–1 series victory.

Sweet Chariot.

THE NEW 7 SEATER SINTRA FROM VAUXHALL

CROSSING THE DIVIDE

BY **DAVID LAWRENSON**

At a time when British Rugby League was taking a hammering at the hands of their Australasian cousins in the World Club championship, the part played by former League players in helping the Lions to a historic series win over South Africa was a small crumb of comfort. Although it is a little fanciful to attribute the Lions' success entirely to the 13-man code, nevertheless the impact of players who had spent time in Rugby League was obvious.

For a hundred years the two codes regarded each other with deep suspicion and inevitably a certain amount of myth grew up. In August 1995 the barriers came down and players were now free to play whatever code they liked. If nothing else, the two cross-code challenge matches between Wigan and Bath in 1996 proved what most sensible observers have known for a long time – that the two games are fundamentally different and should remain so.

Of course that won't stop players from trying both and there will always be those who are more suited to one than the other. The truly great player, like Jonathan Davies, will thrive on any rugby field, but for others the process can be decidedly hit and miss.

It probably takes a special talent to pick out those who will be successful in a new environment, certainly Doug Laughton, the former coach of Widnes and Leeds, believes he has a God-given gift for spotting great rugby players. His record certainly speaks for itself having been responsible for persuading Martin Offiah, Jonathan Davies, Alan Tait, John Devereux, Paul Moriarty, Emosi Koloto, Craig Innes and Jim Fallon to switch codes.

Fran Cotton and Ian McGeechan appear to be similarly gifted for when their squad for South Africa was announced it raised a few eyebrows, not least due to the inclusion of John Bentley and Alan Tait, two players who had arguably spent their best years in League. In fact all the ex-Rugby League players in the Lions' squad performed well, none more so than Scott Gibbs, whose brushing aside of the giant Springbok prop Os du Randt in the second Test will be one of the abiding images of the tour. Rugby League did not make Gibbs a great player, but the time he spent at St Helens certainly helped to hone his skills. Even in his early Rugby Union days with Swansea, Gibbs played like a League player, his love of the physical confrontation and direct running making him a natural for the 13-a-side game. Of all the Union recruits to League over the last decade he was the one who adapted to the game the quickest, relishing in the head-on tackling and the abundant opportunities to run the ball.

It wouldn't be surprising to find that he missed that intensity playing in the Welsh first division, but facing the Springboks was probably little different to taking on Wigan at Central Park. I would not be surprised to see Gibbs go back to St Helens at some point, not for the money but the fun of it – he genuinely likes Rugby League.

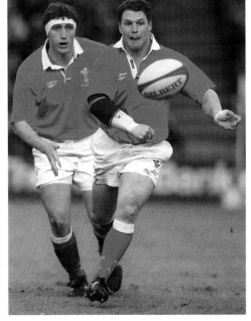

Truly talented players such as Jonathan Davies and Scott Gibbs (below) are able to thrive in both codes of the game.

His Welsh team mate, Allan Bateman, is another convert who seems equally at home in either code. Although not as physical as Gibbs, Bateman is a wonderful footballer with great ball skills and excellent timing. He had a distinguished career at Warrington, but his stature in the game was confirmed when he went to play in Australia and managed to hold a regular first-team place at the mighty Cronulla Sharks in Sydney before moving back to Union with Richmond.

Scott Quinnell looked to be enhancing his reputation as one of the most dynamic forwards in world Rugby Union before his tour was cut short by injury. If he had not gone back to Union, he seemed destined to become a mighty force in Rugby League with Wigan.

Players like Allan Bateman (above) and John Bentley (below) were able to hone their skills in League before returning to Union.

Success for Rugby Union forwards in League is much rarer because the requirements are so different. The specialist skills required for line out and scrummaging are redundant in League where forwards must be good handlers with immense upper-body strength. Quinnell had come to League at a young enough age to develop these attributes which, allied to his natural abilities, were turning him into a real handful in a Wigan jersey. That explosive power and ball-handling ability stood him in good stead in South Africa where Ian McGeechan sought to play a more fluid, open game rather than mixing it in close quarters with the heavier South African packs.

Bentley and Tait were the selections who really came up trumps for Fran Cotton. Bentley has always been a wholehearted performer and was a consistent try scorer with both Leeds and Halifax. Although he made a couple of appearances for Great Britain he probably deserved more, although with flyers like Martin Offiah and Jason Robinson around competition was pretty fierce for the wing positions.

Bentley's direct running and sheer physical presence during his spell back in Union with Newcastle probably convinced Cotton that here was a man who would stand up to any kind of intimidation. Here was a player who could also stay on his feet long enough for the back row to get to him and recycle the ball, vital to McGeechan's overall plan of keeping the heavy Springbok pack moving. In Rugby League, wingers are taught that getting tackled into touch is a cardinal sin because it surrenders possession to the opposition so it was no surprise to see Bentley resisting all efforts to take him over the sidelines in South Africa thus keeping the ball in play and avoiding a line out.

Alan Tait must be thinking he's living in the land of make believe. Twelve months before joining the Lions in South Africa he was playing in the second team at Leeds Rugby League Club and probably contemplating going back to his native Kelso and playing a few games of Union in the twighlight of his career. Doug Laughton brought the Scottish international centre to Widnes and turned him into one of the best attacking full backs around who went on to represent Great Britain 14 times. When Laughton moved to Leeds he brought Tait with him, but when Dean Bell took over Tait did not figure in the new coach's plans and despite the team having one of their worst seasons in their history in 1996, Tait was left languishing in the reserves, making just a handful of first-team appearances. However, a move back to Union with Newcastle revitalised his career and not only did he move back to his old position of centre, but was picked for Scotland and enjoyed a triumphant return which obviously caught the eye of Fran Cotton and Ian McGeechan. Apart from their obvious talents, the ex-Rugby League players in the Lions' ranks probably brought a professional attitude to the party, much needed for the daunting task which lay ahead. After all they had been professional athletes for years playing against other professionals week in week out, which breeds a tough mental attitude. Most of their Lions colleagues had been fully professional for barely a year and were probably still adjusting to rugby as a career.

Martin Offiah, one of Rugby League's deadliest finishers, found the transition harder than most, but would have thrived at a more successful club.

But not every ex-League player has found the transition to Union quite so rewarding. Following his signing from Rosslyn Park in 1987, Martin Offiah became one of the greatest try scorers in the history of Rugby League. His phenomenal pace, athleticism and sheer footballing instinct saw him score many great tries for both Widnes and Wigan, but in 1996 he decided that he wanted a new challenge and switched back to Rugby Union. Although he continues to play League for the London Broncos during the summer, his main contract and commitment is with Bedford Rugby Union club.

Offiah was hoping for an England cap, but he had a tough first season. If he had gone to a top first division club like Wasps or Leciester, things might have been different, but Bedford, having finished bottom of the second division the previous season, were in the process of re-building and it was never going to be easy. He himself struggled with a toe injury at the beginning of the season and it took him a while to adjust to a new side which was changing all the time and a distinct lack of try scoring opportunities.

However, other former League wings, Adrian Hadley at Sale and Jim Fallon at Richmond, benefited from being in successful sides, and their experience as professional rugby players stood them in good stead in their newly professionalised Rugby Union clubs.

All the players so far mentioned had been brought up in the Union game, spending time in League before switching back, but the breaking down of barriers between the two codes also meant that dyed-in-the-wood League players could try Union. A number of players including Henry and Robbie Paul, Gary Connolly and Jason Robinson took short-term contracts with both Bath and Harlequins towards the end of 1996 in what proved an interesting experiment.

Gary Connolly is regarded as one of the best centres in world Rugby League, and his strength, speed and footballing ability meant he adapted well with Harlequins to a game he had never played before.

Robbie Paul found life a little harder at Quins, being a natural scrum half in League but with the scrum half role vastly different in Union, he had to fit in elsewhere in the back line.

Robbie's brother, Henry, spent his time at Bath and once again he found himself being played out of position away from his usual fly half role. Jason Robinson also spent time at Bath. One of the most dangerous broken-field runners in the world, Robinson benefited from having a sympathetic coach at Bath in the shape of Brian Ashton, a Wigan man by birth who knew all about Rugby League.

Despite playing out of position, Henry Paul made a great impact during his time at Bath.

Ashton told the wing to forget about kicking and just to run with the ball, which was fine because Robinson has the speed and elusiveness to succeed most times although playing him at full back on occasions was probably a little too ambitious. Robinson proved a willing pupil and was desperate to learn about how to play the Union game.

The biggest problem confronting League players in Union surrounds the releasing of the ball after the tackle to set up a ruck or maul. There are also differences in positioning and angles of running which don't come naturally to a player brought up on League.

Significantly almost all the players who swap from League to Union are backs and the ones that make the transition easiest are wings and centres because the requirements are the most similar, the biggest differences lie in the forwards.

Few Rugby Union forwards have made a big impact in League, unless they've changed early enough in their careers to learn new skills. But at least League is a fairly straightforward game and if you are strong, mobile and skilful you will do well in the game. However, the same cannot be said of League forwards in Union. The last 12 months has seen several trying their hand and almost without exception they have failed.

The case of Mike Forshaw makes interesting reading. Forshaw was a good second-row forward with Leeds before he went to Saracens during the 1996–97 season, but he couldn't command a regular first-team place and by the end of the season he was back in League. He signed for Bradford and not only managed to establish himself in the best pack in the Super League, but turned in some brilliant performances. Similarly, Richie Eyres, a former Leeds and Great Britain second row, tried his luck with both Sale and Neath before admitting defeat and moving back to Rugby League.

Jason Robinson was an eager student who was desperate to learn about Union.

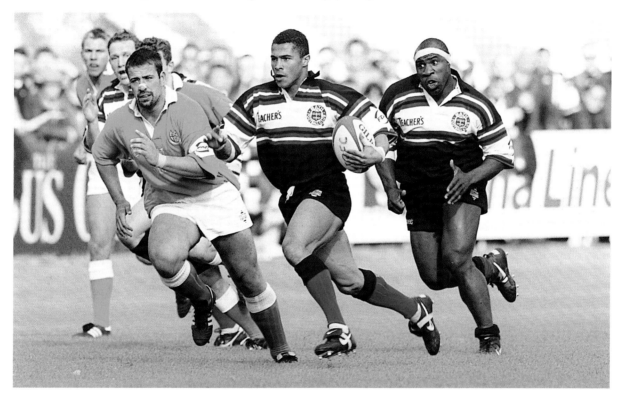

Trying to get the hang of rucks and mauls, let alone line-out jumping is something which is beyond most League forwards who were not born to it. In the Bath versus Wigan clash of the codes under Union laws at Twickenham, no matter how talented the Wigan forwards were, even after several training sessions with Orrell, they could not get to grips with the rucks and mauls and towards the end of the game reverted to basically playing League, moving the ball through the hand at every possible occasion.

The last 12 months have been fascinating for anyone who has interest in both codes and an open mind and it has proved what most sensible observers have thought for a long time – that the codes are very different and although there will always be a certain amount of switching between the two, at top level only the truly great players can hope to play both successfully.

The Heineken Cup – Things you didn't know

- Brive's semi-final against Cardiff in January only went ahead thanks to the efforts of locals. The rugby-mad town in the deep south of France was hit by heavy snow and an army of volunteers worked through the night clearing away 200 tonnes of the stuff. The match went ahead and Brive won 26–13.

- The most bad-tempered match last season was Llanelli against Pau. Three players were given their marching orders for fighting. The Welshman who was sent off, Iwan Jones, should certainly have known better. He's a CID officer.

- Italian Club Treviso may not have done particularly well on the rugby field last season but at least they can take comfort in the thought that they were the best turned out of the 20 teams: their club sponsor is the clothing company Benetton.

But what about the players?

- One of the stars of last season's European Cup was Brive winger Sebastien Carrat. The Frenchman has represented his country in the 100 metres, clocking up a PB of 10.53. Needless to say when he got the ball not many people could catch him.

- Another player who performed wonders last season was Cardiff and British Lions scrum-half Rob Howley. He's a big fan of the tournament and thinks it will help improve the quality of British rugby. It will provide a stage from which we can progress and improve.

- England flanker Lawrence Dallaglio travelled to the land of his father last season when Wasps played Milan. Dallaglio, whose father is Italian, was approached by Milan a few years back after he had played for England Under-21 against their Italian counterparts. Dallaglio stayed in England and is now captain of Wasps.

- Players from the Scottish Borders can claim to have the most diverse range of jobs. They include a farmer, joiner, plumber, fireman, carpet fitter, hosiery worker, mechanical engineer, precision engineer and a knitwear supervisor.

- One of Leicester's star players last season was 20 year-old Leon Lloyd, despite playing with two metal plates in his left arm. The plates were inserted after a horrific car crash on the M1 two years ago. Leon was pulled from the wreckage five seconds before the car blew up.

RUGBY
WORLDWIDE

FIJI TAKE THE WORLD 7s CROWN

BY IAN ROBERTSON

The Cathay Pacific Hongkong Bank 7s has been the outstanding global 7s tournament every year for the past 20 years and it speaks volumes for its success that for one glorious weekend each spring the green oasis of the Government Stadium in the middle of the concrete jungle that is Hong Kong has been the centre of attraction of world rugby.

It was inevitable that one day the World Cup 7s would be held in Hong Kong and that is exactly what happened in March 1997.

Up until last year, the Cathay Pacific Hongkong Bank 7s had always been held over two days and there is absolutely no doubt in my mind that is what should always happen in the future. It has never been very difficult to work out the top six or seven seeds and it has to be said that a quick look at the various qualifying tournaments plus the last three Hong Kong 7s would have made it fairly straightforward to list a top eight seeds followed by the next best eight teams.

From all known information of recent 7s competitions, you did not need to be Einstein to work out that Fiji, New Zealand, Australia, Western Samoa, England and South Africa would fully justify being amongst the top seeds. Throw in any two from France, Korea, Tonga and Hong Kong and you have a most acceptable top eight seeds.

On that basis the tournament could have been decided over two days and it would have avoided dragging out the whole repetitive charade over three days. However, the final day in 1997, as ever, produced some magnificent and memorable rugby. The first two days featuring over 16 hours of rugby had very little to commend them.

Of much greater value earlier in the week was the traditional 10-a-side tournament which attracted a host of famous internationals from the recent past. This list included Gavin Hastings, the former captain of Scotland and the British Lions and for him, playing in the team was just a part of a really active week. At the weekend he was a key member of the ITV television team and on the day he arrived in Hong Kong, on the Monday of 7s week he was one of the star attractions at the biggest and best Gala Dinner of the week.

The Gala Rugby Ball at the magnificent Sheraton Hotel was the perfect start to a great week of rugby. Held in the ballroom of the Sheraton Hotel and masterminded by the manager Ananda Arawwawela and his marketing manager Connie Wong, it turned into one of the best five rugby dinners I have ever been privileged to attend and as I have been to over 1,000 in the last 30 years that puts its huge success in perspective. Special mention must also be made of Des McGahan and his company Prism who helped to market the dinner. Des and Prism have been an integral part of the PR exercise for the Hong Kong 7s for most of the 20 years I have been going and throughout that time I have marvelled at the clinical efficiency and cheerful friendliness they have brought to a very difficult and highly pressurised job.

But back to the dinner. First of all the meal at the Sheraton was the highest quality I can ever recall at a rugby dinner. This put everyone in the best of spirits. There followed two memorable speeches, the first from Gavin Hastings who represented the modern generation of professional rugby players, and who delivered a fund of stories about his days with Scotland and the British Lions.

The other speaker was the legendary Willie John McBride, arguably the most famous northern hemisphere rugby player of all time. He won 63 caps for Ireland and went on five British Lions tours between 1962 and 1974 – a record which will surely never be beaten. He gave an unforgettable speech which was brilliantly funny and yet liberally sprinkled with a few serious points on the state of the game. He received a prolonged standing ovation from the 300 members of the audience.

In between the two speakers an auction was held which raised a staggering £12,000 for various charities including contributions to the Hong Kong Rugby Union Injured Players Fund, the newly formed Hong Kong Caledonian Foundation, and our own Wooden Spoon Society.

This was the first major rugby dinner at the Sheraton Hotel, but it was such a success it will surely be repeated every year. Congratulations to Ananda, Connie and Elaine Joe, the banqueting supremo.

It was, of course, a great night for Wooden Spoon and our executive director David Roberts was delighted to receive a cheque for the best part of £4,000.

After a few visits to the 10s, a few press lunches and dinners and the occasional glass of beer, we reached Friday and the opening day of the World Cup 7s. The idea of the first day was, apparently, to work out a proper seeding list for the second day. As it transpired, there was precious little difference between the two days. On the opening day New Zealand played in a pool with Japan and Tonga. After the seeding committee fed all the day's statistics into the computer on the second day the pool put New Zealand in with Japan and Tonga yet again. Not very imaginative. Similarly, Scotland were pooled with Australia on both days.

It was therefore, very easy to criticise the World Cup organisers for producing two extremely long days of less than riveting rugby on the Friday and the Saturday.

Fortunately, the final day on the Sunday made everything worthwhile with eight hours of truly outstanding, entertaining rugby of the very highest quality followed by a brilliantly orchestrated closing ceremony featuring a local Hong Kong operatic tenor Warren Mok singing 'Amazing Grace' and a Chinese pop star singing her most recent hit.

For the four Home Unions the World Cup was not a great success with only England reaching the quarter-finals of the Cup whilst Scotland and Wales were relegated to the Plate competition on the final day and Ireland fared worst of all losing to Japan in the semi-final of the Bowl.

On the opening day Ireland lost narrowly to Argentina and heavily to South Africa. It was no better for the Irish on the second day with big defeats against South Africa again and Hong Kong. Indeed the only victory Ireland managed was a 33–5 victory over Portugal in the quarter-final of the Bowl.

The Welsh fared a little better. In their pool games they drew with Namibia and lost to Western Samoa on day one before beating Namibia and being trounced by the eventual winners, Fiji, on the second day. They made an early exit on the final day when they lost to Tonga in the quarter-finals of the Plate.

The Scots did much better. They followed up a draw with Australia and a big win over Romania with an even bigger win over Portugal and a defeat by Australia. In the quarter-finals of the Plate, Scotland ran up 43 points against Romania before losing heavily to Hong Kong in the semi-finals.

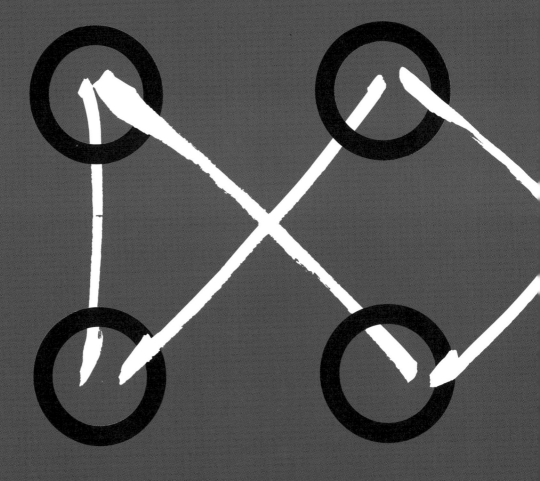

We offer more flights from the UK to Hong Kong than any other ai
China with our sister airline, Dragonair. Cathay Pacific. The Heart

CONNECTIONS

well as the best connections around Asia and also on to 15 cities in

For the record Hong Kong went on to win the Plate with a win over Tonga. In the final of the Bowl, America beat Japan.

However, the focus of attention all weekend was the Melrose Cup – that was the prize for the winners of the World Cup.

The defending champions, England, had looked far and away the best of the northern hemisphere sides and played some very good 7s rugby on the first two days of competition. They won all four of their pool games – two against Canada and one each against Zimbabwe and Cook Islands.

The dejected England players leave the field after their quarter-final defeat at the hands of Western Samoa. England failed to repeat their success of 1993, despite some fine 7s performances – particularly from Chris Sheasby (inset).

Unfortunately in the quarter-finals of the Cup they came up against a very good Western Samoan side and lost by 21 points to 5 to end their involvement in the tournament. Chris Sheasby, who was outstanding in England's World Cup triumph in 1993, had another very good tournament and Neil Back along with Richard Hill in the forwards and Nick Beal in the backs all had their moments. However, at the end of a ridiculously long domestic season, the players looked jaded and the humid conditions as well as the jet lag made it all too difficult.

There were no such problems for the teams from the southern hemisphere and it was no great surprise that four sides who were at the start of their own particular rugby season – Fiji, Western Samoa, New Zealand and South Africa – should all reach the semi-finals.

Fiji achieved this with a win over Korea, South Africa beat France and New Zealand overwhelmed Australia. In the semi-finals Fiji enjoyed a comfortable 38–14 victory over Western Samoa, who had the greatest difficulty winning any possession, and the South Africans had an equally easy route to the final with a 31–7 win over New Zealand.

The final was a wonderful match between two very good sides featuring so many great 7s players. Of course, the star of every one of the previous half-a-dozen Cathay Pacific Hongkong Bank 7s – the brilliantly talented Fijian fly-half Waisale Serevi – was the star yet again. This multi-skilled footballer is a breathtakingly gifted entertainer and with his lethal side-stepping, glorious change of pace and silky running, he dominated the entire tournament. He had first-class support from several indecently capable ball players, notably Lemeki, Marika and Manasa Bari.

Considering that the South Africans play precious little 7s rugby, they did exceedingly well to reach the final of the Cup. They, too, had tremendous natural talent in their team with Joost van der Westhuizen proving to be an inspirational scrum half. The Springbok flanker, André Venter, turned out to be one of the best forwards in the whole competition and they had another potential match winner in the Orange Free State threequarter Stephen Brink.

Fiji captain, Waisale Serevi again proved what a formidable 7s player he could be.

Although the Fijians were the hot favourites to win the final, South Africa made the best possible start when Venter, all power and pace, scored two tries in the first four minutes. Brink added the conversions for a 14–0 lead. The Fijians had not conceded a single point on the first two days scoring 205 points in their matches against Portugal, Hong Kong, Namibia and Wales, and they had won their quarter-final against Korea 56–0. Before the final, they had only conceded two tries against Western Samoa in the semi-final, so it is a handsome tribute to the South Africans that they were able to take such a commanding lead for most of the first half.

But just before half-time, Fiji hit back with a try by Marika which Serevi converted to cut the deficit to 14–7.

Just as South Africa scored two tries in four minutes in the first half, so Fiji did the same in the second half. Serevi provided the magic for Luke and Lemeki to score and Serevi also kicked one conversion. Lemeki scored a fourth Fijian try to make it 24–14 but with just over a minute remaining Brink cut inside after a great break down the touchline to score and he immediately added the conversion. 24–21 to Fiji with just 40 seconds left. South Africa took the restart quickly for one last heroic effort, but they fumbled the ball and Fiji cleared to touch to win the Melrose Cup.

They were the most complete team in the tournament and in Serevi they had the best player. South Africa may be the World Cup champions at 15-a-side rugby, but at 7-a-side it is the Fijians who are the undisputed champions of the world.

(From top left to bottom). The Fiji players show their joy at the final whistle. Waisale Serevi gets a lift from a fan and posing for the cameras – Fiji, seven-a-side champions of the world.

GLENRYCK/HENLEY 7s

BY NIGEL STARMER-SMITH

The Wooden Spoon Society's support of disadvantaged children has justly made this rugby-based charity world-renowned. How fitting then that their direct involvement with rugby should be exemplified at the highest level – with seven-a-side world champions Fiji, decked out in those subtle Wooden Spoon colours! Once the Fiji Spartans (alias Fiji) took to the field at the second annual Glenryck/Henley 7s one knew it was to be a successful day. Both brothers Waisale and (lesser-known) Mell Serevi along with four of the Fiji World Cup-winning seven in Hong Kong in March, were here – it was a display to grace any rugby club ground. Not surprisingly, the unsurpassed skills of the masters of the shortened form of the game left would-be contenders for the Glenryck Trophy, Oxfordshire Cup and £25,000 prize trailing in their wake, despite valiant efforts from the two Oxbridge universities (Cambridge lost the final 52–15 – and to score three tries was no mean feat!) Northampton, Wasps, Durham University and Henley, the hosts, on the path to the final. With the Wooden Spoon Society playing its part in support of the 7s tour by the Fiji Spartans – and the generous sponsorship of the South Sea islanders by both DHL and the Renault Retail Group – so many people were able to see at first-hand the ingredients of the world's greatest exponents of this spectacular art.

The seven-a-side world champions, decked out in Wooden Spoon colours, strolled to victory in the Glenryck/Henley 7s competition.

Acer ◆

FROM
£1,449*
INC. MOBILE PRODUCTIVITY BASE

THE NEW SLIMLINE EXTENSA 900 SERIES.
NOW IT'S EVEN EASIER TO PICK UP
AN EXTRAORDINARY NOTEBOOK.

Only 4.9 lb. That's the weight of our new slimline Extensa 900 series; the slimmest notebooks in their class by far.

Yet light weight doesn't mean losing out on heavyweight 133 MHz Pentium® processor performance – or six hours battery life.

Add our Mobile Productivity Base, and you can add a floppy drive, extra battery, or CD-ROM. And since it adds only 2 lb to the total weight, an Extensa 900 series is still lighter than most of its competitors.

And for once, rapid travel only requires an economy fare. Prices start at just £1,449*.

Extraordinary.

Find out more. Simply call us on 0990 402400.

Extensa 900 CDS

133 MHz Pentium® chip with secondary cache
16 MB EDO RAM (48 MB max.);
2 MB video RAM. 1.35 GB hard disk
12.1" SVGA DSTN display. Windows 95
11.8" x 9" x 1.5". Mobile Productivity Base as standard

Extensa 900 CDT

As Extensa 900 CDS, but 11.3" SVGA
TFT display

Mobile Productivity Base

Modular 8x CD-ROM or floppy
drive
Optional extra lithium-ion battery
APCI slot to free both PC slots for other uses

intel inside

pentium® PROCESSOR

Extensa

Developed with **TEXAS INSTRUMENTS**

THE BIGGEST RUGBY SHOW ON EARTH - Two years and counting

BY CHRIS THAU

The hand-over ceremony of the Rugby World Cup trophy before the first Lions Test in Cape Town was a timely reminder that the 'biggest rugby show on earth' is less than two years away. The countdown to Cymru '99 commenced as soon as the handsome piece of silverware was held aloft by the two senior RWC directors attending the match, RWC chairman Leo Williams and Vernon Pugh QC, who is also chairman of the game's governing body, the IRFB. The trophy returned to the UK, and after the ritual polishing and cleaning in the workshops of the Queen's jewellers, Garrards, re-emerged at a spectacular presentation ceremony in Cardiff, the host city of the 1999 RWC final.

This event, broadcast live by Sky Television, reminded the rugby pundits that the fourth RWC had already kicked off on 26 September 1996, when Latvia beat Norway 44–6 in Riga. It is true, RWC 1999 is not big news yet. The likes of England, Australia, Scotland, Ireland, Western Samoa, and Argentina have yet to enter the qualifying rounds. The early matches involved the lower-ranked European nations: Moldova, Croatia, Luxembourg, Andorra, Ukraine, Hungary, Austria, Switzerland, Israel, Latvia, Norway, Yugoslavia, Lithuania and Bulgaria; RWC newcomers Cook Islands, Tahiti and Papua New Guinea in the Pacific; and Brazil, Bahamas, Barbados and Trinidad and Tobago in the Americas zone. In Asia the ball started to roll with the lower division involving Sri Lanka, Thailand and Singapore.

Yugoslavia, a Serbian team in everything but name, has re-emerged onto the world stage, seriously weakened in the aftermath of the IOC-led boycott. Compared to 1989, the last time they saw RWC action, the Yugoslavs have lost two of their most fertile rugby nurseries, Slovenia and Croatia, the latter spectacularly qualifying to round B of the European zone. The Yugoslav game is now largely confined to five clubs in Belgrade and the Serbian rugby fraternity is making desperate efforts to keep it alive.

Two of the RWC newcomers, Ukraine and Croatia, are establishing themselves as powers to be reckoned with in Continental Europe. Ukraine won their pool undefeated amassing 177 points in the process, and conceding only 21. Mind you, the sternest challenge to the Ukraine's supremacy was provided by the new-look Israeli team, who were desperately unlucky to lose 10–7 to Yugoslavia in Belgrade.

Croatia, coached by Anthony Sumitch, a Croatian of Kiwi stock, and captained by former Montpellier and Le Creusot regular Dragan Lukic, stated their claim to a place in the next round in spectacular fashion. They won all their matches in round A, but equally significant, they helped to re-launch the international career of one of the game's most enduring heroes, former All Black fly half Frano Botica. Botica, who is half Maori/half Croatian recommenced his international career on 17 May 1997, when, watched by his father Nick who had travelled from New Zealand for the occasion, and

The Croatia team line up before their game against Latvia in Split. Frano Botica is seated second from the right.

scores of local relatives, he helped the country of his ancestors win the crucial pool encounter against Latvia in Split.

The third European qualifier, Andorra, with one club and about 40 active senior players – the smallest rugby nation in the world – won their pool undefeated. Their nail-biting 21–20 win over high-flyers Sweden, has secured them pole position in pool three, and with it a rung in round B against top-rated adversaries such as Spain, Portugal, Germany and the Czech Republic. At the opposite end of the spectrum, Hungary beat Luxembourg 12–3 to record their first ever RWC win, while Austria, captained by their ever-enthusiastic No.8 and Austrian Union secretary Dr Christian Schwab, made considerable progress during the past season, despite finishing last in their RWC pool.

In round A of the Pacific Zone, Cook Islands secured its passage to round B thanks to a vital 22–19 win over Papua New Guinea in Raratonga. Having already achieved an elevated World Cup status by reaching the finals of the 1997 RWC 7s in Hong Kong, Cook Islands overcome newcomers Tahiti 40–0 in Papeete to secure themselves a place in round two of the Pacific Zone against World Cup veterans Fiji and Tonga, where their third-division international status was cruelly exposed as they lost both encounters by substantial margins. However, there are many New Zealanders of Raratongan descent (the Bachop brothers are just an example) waiting to be discovered, and one should not rule out the emergence of a new Polynesian power – once the selection policy and priorities are reviewed.

In the Americas group, Trinidad and Tobago made an early impact by dispatching Brazil 41–0 in Port of Spain, but Mike Peter's colleagues were denied a further encounter in pool one when Guyana withdrew, unable to fulfil the fixture. In the other pool, Bermuda, who saw RWC action against the USA in the qualifying rounds of the 1995 RWC, had the chance to sample the sweet taste of success against Barbados and Bahamas. Trinidad and Tobago and Bermuda are taking on the powerful Chilean team in October for a place in round C.

The Asian pool was won predictably by Sri Lanka, but a greatly improved Singapore side gave the Sri Lankans a good run for their money before going down 18–15 at the end of March. For security reasons the match, originally scheduled for Colombo, was played in Kuala Lumpur in Malaysia. Sri Lanka take on Taiwan and Malaysia in round B.

Finally, in Africa, the Arabian Gulf are stealing the headlines. Paul Turner's team managed to win both its matches against RWC debutantes Zambia and Botswana, the former after a thrilling seven-try 30–44 spectacular in Luanshya in the Zambian Copper Belt, and the latter, 53–13, after an impressive display of running rugby in Bahrain. Botswana lost 13–20 to the Zambian visitors, in what was the first-ever match between the two African unions.

The Zambian players map out their strategy during the half-time break in their match against The Gulf.

The advent of professionalism has had a shattering impact on the game and its structure. Financially, the gap between the haves and have-nots has widened. In the current market-place the whole process of developing the game worldwide, something which is being actively pursued by the IRFB, depends on the commercial success of RWC tournaments. This is why the game's leading administrator, IRFB chairman Vernon Pugh is adamant that the RWC, for all its valuale impact on playing standards, is still a means to an end.

'This is the first RWC involving the whole IRFB membership. Over 100 matches are played in the qualifying rounds between nations keen to upgrade their standing and standards. However, for all its public success, phenomenal television ratings and overall attraction, RWC is the game's main fundraiser. RWC is as much a shop window for the game as it is a commercial exercise. The world rugby revolution, triggered off by the RWC, is about to commence,' said Mr Pugh.

'In order to accelerate the development of the game worldwide and to reflect the continual improvement in playing standards, the governing body has decided to increase the size of the tournament from 16 to 20 nations. As a consequence, the 1999 RWC tournament, will be bigger and more competitive than anything ever seen before,' he added.

The days when the big eight – the IRFB founding Unions (England, Scotland, Ireland, Wales, New Zealand, Australia, South Africa and France) – could lie happily in the knowledge that their position and priviledges were secure are gone. For the first time in the short history of the RWC, one of the Home Unions, Wales, was forced to enter the qualifying rounds of the 1995 tournament. England, Scotland, Ireland and Australia followed suit in the following World Cup. The momentum generated by the RWC is gathering pace.

'The success of emerging nations such as Western Samoa, Italy, Argentina and Canada, and the clear potential displayed by Romania, Tonga, Uruguay, RSA and Fiji, has given the RWC credibility. It showed that the RWC is a meritocratic event after all, in which quality and hard work are rewarded. Some of the aspiring nations felt that given time and resources, they could eventually match the top nations. Other unions used the opportunity to test their limited playing potential and identify their relative position on the world rugby scale. There is no doubt that the RWC has acted as a catalyst to many of the changes in the game. As a consequence we have a better game and a brighter future,' siad RWC chairman Leo Williams.

Meanwhile, preparations have started in Wales for the final of the 1999 RWC tournament. The Welsh Rugby Union has appointed former Wales captain and full back Paul Thorburn as tournament director. Thorburn is a member of Cymru '99, the WRU committee in charge of the event which comprises senior members of the WRU general committee including Ron Jones, a former RWC regional director in 1991, Sam Simon and Howard Watkins.

Things are moving ahead at full speed. A total of 41 games will be played in the tournament, which will start and end in Cardiff. The 1999 RWC will be the biggest single sporting event held in the UK since the 1966 Soccer World Cup: travel arrangements need to be made for over 1,000 playing and coaching personnel, referees, and over 2,000 media men from all over the world, not to mention the expected tens of thousands of fans following their favourite team. The opening match and the final will be played at the new Millennium Stadium, Cardiff Arms Park – an astounding high-tech facility with a capacity of 73,500.

A bird's eye view of the work taking place on Cardiff Arm's Park. The new re-developed stadium will have a capacity of 73,500.

LED TO THE SLAUGHTER
– England in Australia

BY KERRI MULDOON AND IAN ROBERTSON

Following their two wins over France at the end of June, Australia fell from grace with a resounding thump when they took on the All Blacks in Christchurch at the beginning of July. New Zealand took complete control in the first half and rattled up a comfortable lead which they seemed content to sit on in the second half.

In simple terms this meant that France, the Grand Slam champions of Europe, could be placed no higher than third in a three-cornered battle with Australia and New Zealand. Once again, it proved that winning the Five Nations championship was one thing, but winning a match in the southern hemisphere against one of the top three countries was something else.

What it certainly goes to show is that when all four of the Home Unions combine to form the British Lions they can scale the heights and win Test matches in the southern hemisphere, as they did in South Africa, but the individual Unions never seem to fare too well on their own.

While France were being put in their place in Australia, Scotland found the going very difficult at provincial level in South Africa, losing more games than they won without even playing a Test.

The final piece in the 1997 jigsaw came in the middle of July when England landed in Australia to play a one-off Test against the Wallabies. England had finished runners-up in the Five Nations capturing the Triple Crown *en route*, so hopes were high that they might restore the reputation of the northern hemisphere in this first Test for the new Cook Trophy – part of a five-year deal in which England and Australia are to meet twice

The two sides line up for the game in which many think England had no chance of winning.

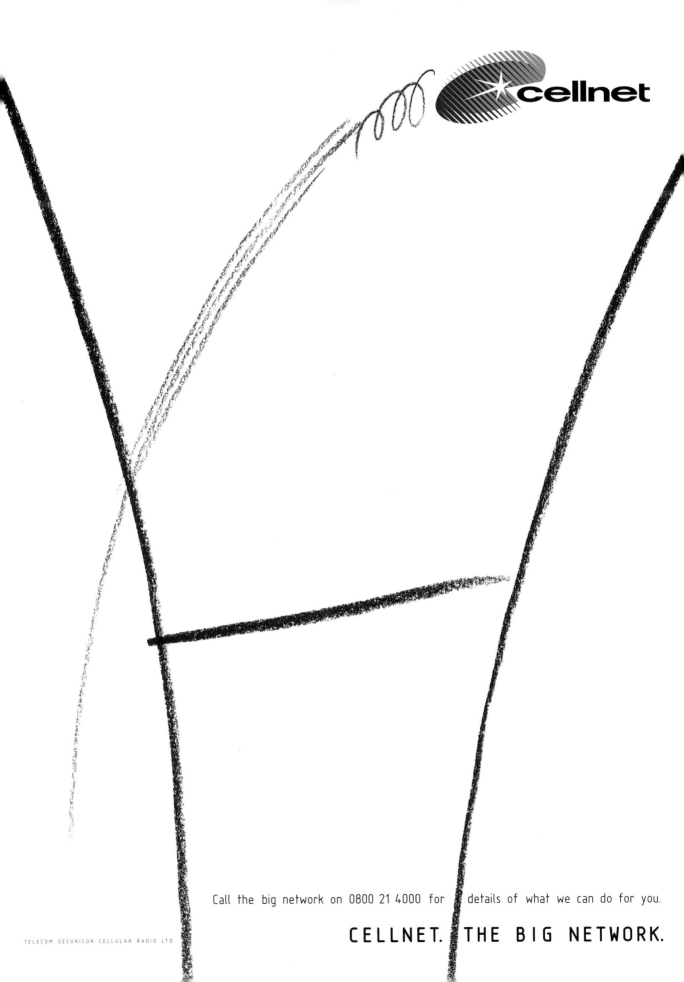

cellnet

Call the big network on 0800 21 4000 for details of what we can do for you.

CELLNET. THE BIG NETWORK.

a year, with a July game in Australia and a November fixture at Twickenham.

The reality of the situation was totally at odds with the pre-match blurb. The truth was that England had precious little chance of winning as the timing of the fixture was unbelievably awful. Indeed, if the RFU had taken out a calender and chosen the worst possible weekend of the entire year to play a Test in Sydney, then there is absolutely no doubt in my mind that the date they would have chosen was 12 July. The RFU actually agreed to play on the day that gave England the least possible chance of winning.

Conversely, the match came at a perfect time for Australia. Their Test players had just completed two months of Super 12 rugby followed by three full Test matches against France and New Zealand. The England players, on the other hand, were at the very end of the longest season of their careers. They had been playing non-stop rugby from the

end of August 1996 right through to 5 July 1997 without a weekend off. Forty-six weeks with no break obviously took its toll, but that is only half of the story. The England players on the Lions tour (12 were to play against Australia) then had to endure a 15-hour flight from Johannesburg to Sydney on the Monday night after the third Test which arrived at 9pm in Sydney on the Tuesday evening just 95 hours before they faced Australia.

Then these players had to adjust to the worst debilitating factor of all – the eight-hour time difference between Johannesburg and Sydney. If that were not enough to completely scupper their chances, there were other factors to be taken into account which further

Matt Dawson stops the forward drive of Joe Roff. The English defence helped to keep them in the game until their bodies could give no more .

diminished their already negligible chances. Firstly, on 5 July in Johannesburg they were playing at an altitude of 6,000 feet – in Sydney they were at sea level. Secondly, the RFU agreed to an 8pm floodlit kick-off which would guarantee the players would be able to offer the least resistance. The fact that England slumped to their third biggest defeat in 20 Tests against Australia should have come as no surprise to anyone. The odds were stacked against them.

As it was Australia did not play all that well and at half-time, having spent 40 minutes on the attack, they only led 8–3. They made a lot of handling mistakes and their captain John Eales missed four goal kicks from five attempts. He did manage one penalty and full back Matt Burke exploded into the line to score a try for a lead of 8–0 midway through the half, but outstanding English defence kept Australia at bay.

Just before half-time, Tim Stimpson kicked a penalty and after half-time Mike Catt dropped a goal to cut the deficit to 8–6. But then England found dragging exhausted, jet-lagged bodies round the field at international pace in the final 20 minutes was too much for them, and the Australians, without playing particularly well, ran in three more tries – Tune, Gregan and Horan were the scorers.

Perhaps the most frightening statistic of all is the fact that by the time the players landed back in England after 10-and-a-half months of solid rugby they would have a three- or four-week break before embarking on pre-season training with their clubs in preparation for the new season just a fortnight later. In a fierce, physical contact sport like rugby this is unrealistic, unacceptable and, indeed, outrageous.

John Eales raises the Cook Trophy – for England a chance for revenge will come in November when the Australians visit Twickenham.

The question is why did it happen in the first place. The answer is very simple – money. Professional sport is all about money and it has not taken professional rugby very long to adapt and cash in. The reason England were led to the slaughter in Sydney in July is because when Australia play the return leg at Twickenham in November, the RFU are guaranteed a sell-out crowd with gate receipts in excess of £2,000,000.

The word is that in the summer of 1998 it is the intention of the RFU to embark on an even crazier itinerary. It beggars belief, but there is a plan to play the USA in Los Angeles, followed by two Tests and provincial games in New Zealand before flying to Australia for the first leg of the Cook Trophy and then on to South Africa for a Test match against the Springboks.

The All Blacks would reject such an itinerary as out of hand, and let's hope the RFU see sense and do likewise. To undertake so much travelling with so many time differences is madness. The plea must surely be to give the multi-talented England players a chance to do themselves justice. That was most definitely not the case in 1997.

By the autumn of 1997 the world pecking order was reasonably straightforward. The British Lions and New Zealand would have to share the top spot, with South Africa and Australia in contention for third and fourth position. Then there would be a bit of a gap before France in fifth position and after another gap, England in sixth place. Wales, Scotland and Ireland would bring up the rear in a list of the major countries.

THE MAJOR TOURS

BY **BILL MITCHELL**

Jonathan Davies says farewell to an old friend. Australia's tour to France and the UK signalled the end of a glittering international career for David Campese.

A s usual there were several incoming tours during the period pre-Christmas 1996 and by far the best and most successful involved the Australians, who went through a dozen fixtures and won them all – the first time they had achieved this feat in Europe. They did this inspite of the fact that they suffered badly from injuries and were never able to field their best side in any of the important matches. The tour also saw the last of David Campese on the international scene.

There were international victories against Italy, Scotland, Ireland and Wales and only in Dublin were they really under any pressure before pulling away. There was controversy about the final match, which was against a weakened Barbarians side, because they felt that England would have been more suitable opponents. It was explained that arrangements for the Barbarians were too well underway for a change to be made, but in many ways it was a pity that it could not be done.

Arwel Thomas dives into the corner to score a consolation try for Wales during their defeat against an impressive South Africa.

Western Samoa were also here in November and December 1996 and won eight matches out of 11, defeats coming in a somewhat casual fashion against Saracens, Llanelli and Bath. Their high spot was a 40–25 (four tries to one) victory over Ireland in Dublin, something which said much about their continued progress on the international scene – and something, too, about the decline in the Irish game.

South Africa 'A' came in November and December and lost only two matches – to the 'A' teams of Scotland and Ireland. They countered this by beating England 'A' and Emerging Wales amongst their nine successes, but most of their opposition was of a poor standard with English clubs refusing to release players.

The senior South African side was involved in a full international tour, which started in Argentina with four victories including comfortable Test successes in Buenos Aires. Five games were then played in France and defeats were suffered against the French Barbarians and French Universities, but three other games were won including both Tests by margins of 22–12 and a nailbiting 13–12. A swift visit to Wales produced an entertaining and occasionally boisterous match, but the Springboks won 37–20. On this showing it seemed that the British Lions would be severely pressed to win any Tests in South Africa in 1997. How wrong can one be?

(Above) The progress
of German Llanes is
stopped by Simon
Shaw and Tim Rodber
during Argentina's
clash with England.
(Right) Justin Marshall
feeds the ball to his
threequarters as the
New Zealand Barbarians
take control at
Twickenham.

Argentina's seven games in November and December produced five hollow victories against four weak sides and a brave Combined Services outfit. England 'A' won a close encounter, 22–17, and the tour ended at Twickenham with a narrow 20–18 defeat.

Queensland were here at the same time and might well have emulated their senior Wallaby countrymen with a 100 per cent record had they not lost their prop Ryan to a stupid offence after they had taken the lead against Cambridge University at the beginning of the game. They lost that one in the end, but won their seven remaining matches ending up with a 25–22 victory over England 'A' – a clear sign that Australian rugby has a sound basis of strength.

The New Zealand Barbarians had made a brief visit to England late in November 1996 and beat a woefully weak Northern Division side 80–0, the various clubs having made sure that the visitors would not encounter any competition before meeting England's full side at Twickenham a few days later, but the home team after briefly holding a second-half lead was ultimatelty trounced with a try by replacement fly half Carlos Spencer, the highlight of the match.

Olo Brown powers his way forwards during Auckland Blues' visit to the Harlequins.

Spencer's province, Auckland, paid Europe a short visit early in 1997 and won its three matches against Bristol (62–21), Harlequins (a close 33–29) and Heineken Cup winners Brive in France (a massive 47–11), but Otago and the United States had already preceded them with the former winning all their seven matches including a comfortable success over England 'A'.

The Americans only played three games in Wales with Pontypridd (15–13) their only victims. Neath (39–15) and the national side (34–14) at Cardiff Arms Park were both far too strong.

In the European close season the main news came from the British Lions' successful tour of South Africa, which is covered elsewhere in this book, but there was also a cameo visit from Scotland, who had mixed results with three victories from six matches – all against strong opposition. Their top performances were victories over Zimbabwe, Northern Transvaal (who had beaten the Lions and fielded a side of similar strength) and Eastern Province. Despite suffering many injuries, the tour will no doubt prove to be a valuable exercise.

This is more than can be said for the visit to New Zealand by an Irish Development party, which won only one match in six and also lost badly to Western Samoa. Argentina played five matches in New Zealand winning only one and suffering a heavy defeat at the hands of the All Blacks in the Test.

Even France were unable to match the success of the Lions and their trip to Australia provided only three wins in six games with defeats in the two Tests against the Wallabies, which would all seem to confirm the view that not only did the Lions do superbly well to leave South Africa with such a good playing record, but also that the southern hemisphere sides are still in the ascendancy.

FACING THE FUTURE WITH NOKIA.

Nokia Telecommunications is at the forefront of tomorrow's technology, developing the solutions to meet the needs of the next generation.

Nokia believes in encouraging achievement, and has built its business on respecting and caring for people, whether customers or suppliers, staff or friends. In our own way we each help to build a better future for everyone, and as part of this Nokia is happy to support the work of The Wooden Spoon.

NOKIA
CONNECTING PEOPLE

Nokia Telecommunications Ltd, Lancaster House, Lancaster Way, Ermine Business Park, Huntingdon, Cambs PE18 6XU, U.K.
Telephone +1480 434444 Fax +1480 435111

CLUBS AND CUPS

The two major influences on Sale over recent years. Paul Turner (right) introduced a new style of open rugby to the club which saw them secure fourth place in division one. John Mitchell (below) added that which many thought was missing – steel. Last season saw them as losing finalists in the Pilkington Cup final and finishing fifth in the league.

take the club storming into division one by playing highly entertaining, but high-risk rugby.

Under his tutellage the players ran the ball from anywhere. They passed behind their backs, they passed behind their legs and centre Jos Baxendell has even been known to head the ball on occasions.

Of course everyone said, 'How wonderful, but what a terrible cropper they'll come in division one.' How wrong they were. 'Tiny' Turner led his side to fourth spot and they rounded off the season by becoming one of the few sides to beat Bath at Bath. The club seemed to be making a habit of it.

The following year they finished fifth and concluded with a draw at Bath after being hopelessly adrift until Turner had put himself on as a second-half replacement.

But the happy days were over. Not everyone liked Paul's man-management style and wheels started to turn, disharmony ran through the club and, in a pretty cock-handed fashion, officials showed Paul the door. He wasn't going without a fight and the club was thrown into the most acrimonious period in its history. The club was split as some threw their weight behind the officials while others, many of them newcomers attracted by the wizardry, backed Paul.

It was a bitter fight. The officials won, just, and Paul went off to Bedford. The pundits had another field day and marked Sale down for relegation again.

They miscalculated badly because they had not taken into account Paul's last noble act. While in Bermuda for the annual jamboree for ageing and ex-internationals, Paul had run into John Mitchell, the man who had skippered Waikato to a record victory over the British Lions during the 1993 tour to New Zealand. The idea had been that Mitchell would join Sale as coaching assistant. Instead he came as number one and gave the side the one thing it lacked. Steel.

He encouraged the flamboyant style, although players were told there was a time and a place for such things, and honed his limited squad of a handful of full-time professionals and part-timers into a more-than-useful outfit.

Suddenly, nobody took Sale lightly and

Harlequins may still have nightmares, having lost to the Cheshire set three times during the season.

If Turner was an inspiration in one sense, Mitchell was a major inspiration in other ways. He was a tough taskmaster, but the players were prepared to run though a brick wall for him.

Recognition may have been slow in coming at Heywood Road but it arrived eventually. Jim Mallinder, David Rees, Jos Baxendell, John Fowler, Dave Baldwin and Steve Diamond were all called up for the England tour to Argentina. Tom Beim and new signing Chris Murohy were called up for the National Under 21 squad.

The only disappointment for Sale was Leicester. The mighty Midlanders seem to have had their mark on Sale in recent seasons and they ran true to form last season. The end of season draw at Heywood Road in the league gave Leicester, rather than Sale, the final European spot. And, at Twickenham, the Leicester pack ruled the roost and made sure of one trophy, even if the rugby was of poor quality.

But Sale have been to Twickenham now. They have had a taste of the icing on the rugby cake and they plan to be back.

A taste of things to come as Sale as they celebrate their Pilkington Cup semi-final victory over Harlequins.

For the " Law Firm of the Year " it's not the Circle Line you want - it's the Main Line.

You could be forgiven for thinking that a visit to the "Law Firm of the Year" means a trip to the City. But think again.

Because the 1997 Law Firm of the Year is Birmingham's Wragge & Co, the largest single office practice outside London.

Our strategy of developing a truly national law firm from a single location has now been recognised by an independent panel of senior legal and business figures.

It is a strategy, they say, which "combines a national reputation with local service". A strategy which makes for "the delivery of a seamless service to clients". And a strategy based on "market specialisation and industry expertise".

But don't just take the experts' word for it. Come and judge us for yourself. In Birmingham.

For more details contact John Crabtree, Senior Partner, on 0121 233 1000.

55 Colmore Row, Birmingham B3 2AS

RICHMOND RFC –
The success formula

BY **TOM KINGSTON**

The challenge of achieving 'back to back' promotions was always going to be a difficult one, notwithstanding the influx of talent at the Athletic Ground last summer. A very close-knit and committed side had gained promotion in April 1996, and it was fair to say that although capable of competing in division two, promotion with the existing squad would have been impossible.

However, the spirit within the club needed to be maintained and, therefore, while seeking to strengthen the squad, the importance lay in 'enhancing' not 'replacing' that which was already here.

The key to achieving success last season lay in ensuring that the undoubted talents of the internationals newly recruited into the club, interacted quickly with the established team spirit within the side. It was this goal which was always at the front of my mind when considering who to bring in.

At the time, with the new professional era only just upon us, very few players were under contract and there were several opportunities available. Gradually, a quality squad was assembled.

An intensive week at a training camp in South West France followed and this proved to be a tremendous success with the 'old' and 'new' merging to become simply Richmond.

The fixture list was not particularly friendly. We had Coventry, Bedford and Newcastle (our serious rivals for promotion) in the first four games. Although, one win and two draws from these three games was at the time a bit disappointing, avoiding defeat proved, on reflection, to be the most significant thing.

It was pleasing that throughout the season so many of the old team contributed so fully to the successes, with 38 players actually playing in the league campaign. Our injury list at times was crippling, but I always believed we had a squad with a much greater depth than our rivals – and so it proved.

In losing only one league game all season, Richmond were promoted in April as worthy champions, scoring a record number of points for the club in the process.

People have asked me when I felt promotion was likely, and without ever wishing to provide the dreaded 'kiss of death', I suspect it was when we beat Coventry at home in such convincing fashion at the end of December, the week

Richmond captain Ben Clarke stops Newcastle's Western Samoan, Pat Lam, in his tracks. New imports blended with the old guard to take Richmond to the top of the second division and to earn a place amongst rugby's élite.

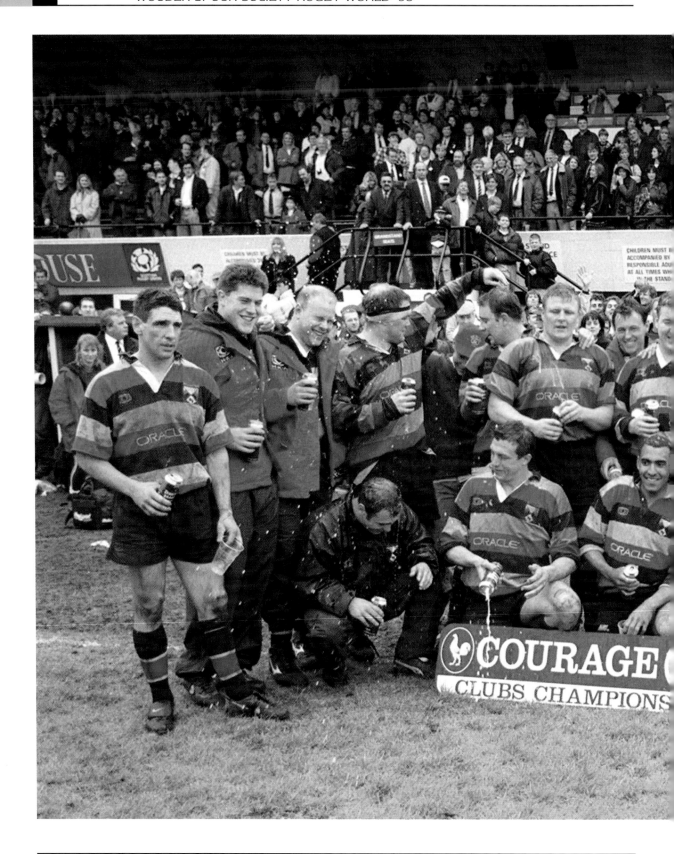

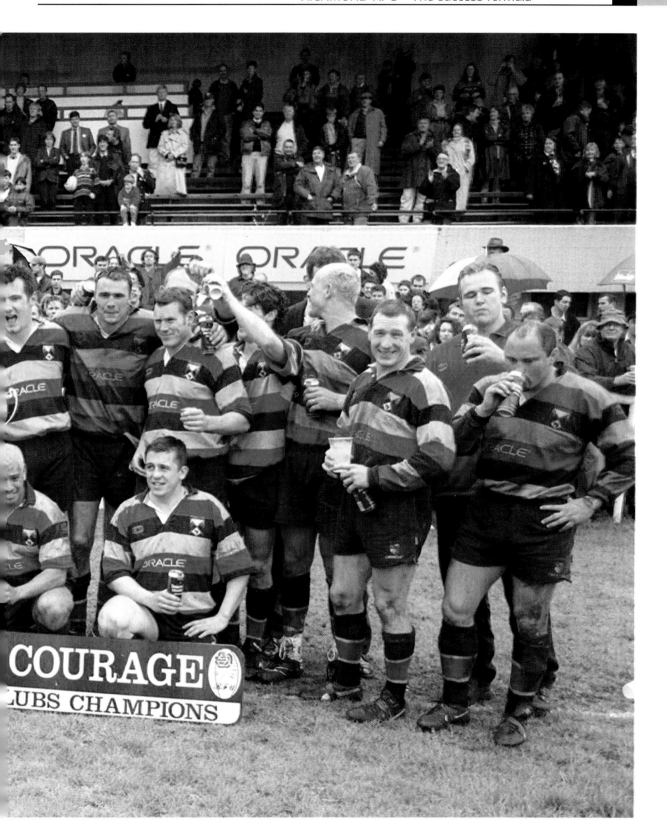

(Previous page) The Richmond squad celebrate their league triumph. (Below) Allan Bateman holds the Courage League Division Two championship trophy aloft.

after losing so narrowly to Sale in the Pilkington Cup. The manner of the defeat at Sale proved to all at Richmond that we were capable of matching the best and the subsequent signings of Steve Atherton from South Africa and Earl Va's from Western Samoa were essentially the start of our recruitment drive for the 1997–98 season.

Anyone who watched the game at Sale would agree that Richmond more than matched the division one side, but the challenge now lies in being able to lift our game to that level every week. There will be no easy games in the top flight.

Once again, I believe strength in depth is going to prove vital and so in the last months I have sought to adopt an active recruitment drive bringing in further quality international players from all over the world. As last summer, the secret to success will lie in our ability to mix the newcomers with the existing players who, incidentally, are all staying at the club.

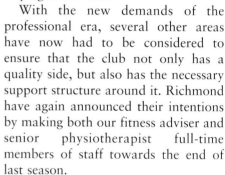

With the new demands of the professional era, several other areas have now had to be considered to ensure that the club not only has a quality side, but also has the necessary support structure around it. Richmond have again announced their intentions by making both our fitness adviser and senior physiotherapist full-time members of staff towards the end of last season.

A full-time youth academy officer has now been recruited with 'scouts' employed across the country to identify talented schoolboys. Gradually a system is being put in place to ensure that Richmond are able to develop the best young players in the country. Our youngsters within the club have already been exposed to technical expertise on both a physical and mental level, which we believe will ultimately allow 18- to 19-year-olds to play at the highest level – something which has not always been the case in the northern hemisphere.

So much for the future. A fascinating season lies in store for Richmond as a newly promoted club in division one. How well we fair once again will come down to that good, old fashioned virtue called team spirit. If, as a club, we remember where we came from and stick together, I am certain that even more exciting times lie around the corner.

THANET RFC – It's Not Over 'Til We Say It's Over

BY **GREG BAYNE**

The Inaugural RFU Intermediate Cup:
Thanet Wanderers 21 Doncaster 13

The first Intermediate Cup final on 3 May 1997 did not run to form. Doncaster were firm favourites, having gone all season unbeaten, and Thanet were true underdogs despite losing only two games themselves, having gone close to the wire in most of their cup games in the run up to the final.

Prior to Christmas, few people in Thanet were concerned about this competition. They narrowly beat Betteshanger, demolished Chichester and saw off the challenge of Old Beccehamians and Lewes. It was not until they routed St Ives in front of a massive home crowd at St Peters that Thanet believed that a trip to Twickenham was possible. Club captain Tom Carlier summed it up. 'We were concentrating on our league games and then we realised that we were unlikely to play many stronger sides in the cup. A trip to Twickenham was definitely within our sights.' Three games later, with Cinderford and Sudbury going to extra-time, Thanet were in the final.

Having reached their goal, Thanet were faced with organising from scratch a grand outing for players and supporters to rugby's HQ. All season long, support had grown and St Peters recreation ground soon became the place to be when the Wanderers were at home. Christened 'The House of Pain' many seasons ago, visiting teams have always been given a 'warm' welcome. An action committee was formed and plans were laid. Having decided on chartering a train for supporters, the demand quickly rose, a second was ordered and then in the last week, a third. Over 4,500 tickets were ordered from Twickenham for the Wanderers supporters. On the day, the total gate for both games was around 10,000, so the depth of the Wanderers support can truly be gauged in those figures.

For the first-team squad, it was planned to be business as usual, with some extra attractions. The team left the clubhouse at 9.30, sent on their way by a local school jazz band. A scheduled stop was made for breakfast, and time was taken for some interviews with the local television station. They were soon on the road again, the squad split into two camps, the *Question of Sport* back-seaters and the 'Thrilla in Manila' video-watchers.

Thanet arrived earlier than planned, at about 12.30. They were quickly ushered into the visitors changing room. Afterwards some players remarked that it was a strange experience. The changing rooms are very large, but devoid of character. They could have been anywhere, but it suddenly dawned on them that many famous bums had sat where they now sat. With plenty of time before the start, the players went out to enjoy some of the Junior final and wave to friends and family in the ever-growing section of the Wanderers crowd. Despite all the recent improvements, Twickenham still remains a ground where you can pick out a familiar face in the crowd from wherever you may be.

At 12.30, the Junior Cup final went into extra-time and the scheduled timetable collapsed. Team photos were taken in the tunnel entrance whilst the junior game was still on. Returning to the changing room, Thanet's players remained remarkably focused. Jokes and banter went back and forth. Tom Carlier's team talk was made and suddenly they were out there on hallowed ground.

Most of the players remarked that the game was a blur and they could remember little. It was a great game, both sides defended well and from the start It was clearly going to be a close match. In the stands all that could be seen was a sea of blue and gold and the cry 'Wann-derrr-errrs!', was incessant and mesmerising.

Running true to past games, Thanet conceded early points and at half-time they were losing. A tactical substitution, Mick Pond for right wing Elliot Stokes, proved inspirational. A move down the right wing broke down on the half-way line and Pond off-loaded the ball to centre Peter Macauley. He outpaced his cover and faced with only the full back to beat, he adeptly chipped him and touched down to score Thanet's first try. On *Rugby Special* the next day, John Inverdale commented that viewers should watch closely as 'not many better tries have been scored at Twickenham this season'. Thanet conceded a penalty immediately after the restart, and Doncaster regained the lead 13–11.

Thanet's players doubled their efforts and when a Doncaster attack broke down in the Thanet 22, full back Gareth Redmond pounced on a loose ball and suddenly found himself with some space to run. He sprinted away and drew the Doncaster full back, passing to wing-forward substitute Simon Harris. With a Doncaster defender on his shoulder, Harris passed left to winger Mario Meyer. 'All I could think about,' said Meyer, 'was to cross the line and get as close to the posts as I could.' Redmond converted to take the Wanderers to 18–13. Doncaster looked completely played out and Thanet clearly were in the ascendancy. With the last kick of the game, Redmond made the final score 21–13. The stewards stood little chance as the pitch was invaded with some panache by Thanet supporters.

Thanet Wanderers captain Tom Carlier raises the RFU Intermadiate Cup to the Twickenham crowd.

The tears were flowing as the cup was raised aloft. The team had come from behind again to win. Thanet catch phrase, 'It's not over 'til we say it's over', had come true again when it mattered most. One unknown supporter was heard to say, 'This is the best day of my life!' It was only 5pm and he was married with two kids! Who knows what the night had in store.

For the players it was obvious what lay in store – a post-match reception and lots of beer. There were a few choruses of 'Sloop John B' with the Doncaster players, and then they joined their supporters on the last train out of Twickenham station for the real sing-song. Their place in rugby history was guaranteed.

HARPENDEN RFC –
Nine steps to glory

BY MICHAEL PARKE

Harpenden Rugby Football Club saw dreams come true at Twickenham on Saturday 3 May 1997 with a win that will go down in history.

Some 2,000 ecstatic supporters watched as Club captain Chris Wright went up to collect the prestigious RFU Junior Cup at the end of a hard fought match against Crewe and Nantwich. He had made it his personal crusade to get the side to Twickenham and had been the driving force throughout the campaign. What a cruel twist of fate it was that he was denied appearing on the field, and what a loss it was to the side, breaking his foot in the very last second of the final game that clinched the league championship for the club. He was a proud man on the day when he hobbled up the famous Twickenham steps with the accolade of the supporters ringing in his ears, to receive the trophy. Harpenden had succeeded where two other Hertfordshire sides had previously faltered, surmounting the final hurdle and bringing the cup to the county for the first time. Glory for the club and the county.

This was not only the biggest occasion in the club's 75-year history, but came hot on the heels of their league championship victory (for the second year in succession) and their winning the Hertfordshire Merit Table. This, coupled with the fact that they were last year's County 7s champions, and their Colts had this year won the County Cup, makes the 1996–97 season the best ever for the club. The match saw some incredibly exciting moments with the lead changing hands several times before Harpenden went on to clinch a 34–31 victory in extra time.

Opposed by a side intent on keeping the game tight and playing to their much bigger, stronger pack, Harpenden stuck to their task and did not desert their adventurous running game – their trademark throughout the campaign. They had done their homework well, decided on their tactics and stuck to them resolutely. Their fitness and persistence told. The forwards, after initial setbacks which saw the side go 13–3 behind in the first quarter of an hour, began to win enough ball to feed the talented threequarter line who had defended magnificently. The Harpenden tactics were triumphant on the day and helped to create an incredibly exciting game.

The Road to Twickenham
A Dream Fulfilled – Nine steps to Glory!

1: A hospital casualty. Harpenden 130 Royal Hospitals 3
A good start to the campaign albeit against weak opposition, with Colts winger Stuart Ramage scoring four tries. The dream begins to take shape.

2: Hedehogs squashed. Harpenden 58 Hitchin 3
Hitchin, known as 'The Hedgehogs', are well and truly trounced as the threequarters run rampant on a surfeit of possession provided by a fine forward display, with McPherson, Tony Baxter, Nick Sinfield, Ian Hamilton, Dave Talbot and Dave Horsley all scoring.

3: A right Cornish past(y)ing. Harpenden 45 London Cornish 11

Against a competent side the threequarters flourish yet again with the forwards dominating and providing a lot of possession. Simon Smith scores a hat-trick and Ian Hamilton, Dean Ford, Nick Sinfield and Andy McPherson all get on the score sheet.

4: Feltham Flounder. Harpenden 37 Feltham 5

The campaign really gains momentum with the threequarters, superbly served by the forwards, again in scintillating form. Simon Smith scores another hat-trick with Ian Hamilton and Dan Phillips also scoring. The loss of fly half Dean Ford (the side's goal kicker) does nothing to stop the accumulation of points. Substitute James 'Jimbo' Cartmel, the Colts captain, shows that he has great ability as a play-maker and goal kicker.

5: Seasiders taken by storm and blown away. Harpenden 66 Felixstowe 5

This significant and comprehensive victory over a side favoured by many to go far gives notice that Harpenden really mean business in the competition and the dream is fast becoming a reality. The pack takes them on up front and the side plays a 15-man game. Powerful scrummaging ensures good possession and the threequarters notch up another six tries. Simon Smith and Tony Baxter score two each and Nick Sinfield and Dave Talbot also score, as does second row Dave Horsley and the back-row partners of Andy McPherson and Dan Phillips. A momentous performance.

Injured Harpenden captain Chris Wright gets his moment of glory as he climbs the famous Twickenham steps to receive the RFU Junior Cup.

6: Tonbridge tamed. Harpenden 29 Tonbridge 14

A visit to fancied Tonbridge gives Harpenden their hardest game to date in the competition. The team, particularly the forwards, are not at their best. Nevertheless they have too much for the men from Kent and are clear victors after leading only 8–6 at half-time. Simon Smith scores twice and Dave Talbot and Tony Baxter also score. Well on course now!

7: That's your lot Folks. Harpenden 30 Folkestone 6

Folkestone, the southern favourites, favoured by many to get to the final after losing out narrowly last year in the semi-final are well beaten by a combination of effort, skill and well thought-out tactics. Over 1,000 spectators watch them fall to Harpenden in the last eight of the competition. The pre-match homework pays off. Attacking their strength, Harpenden's forwards achieve a dominance which doesn't allow Folkestone to get off the back foot and play their usual game. Simon Smith continues his fine scoring spree in the competition and Dave Talbot adds two more with further tries by Nick Sinfield and Rob Humphrey. Beating this much fancied side means Harpenden are well on course. The dream is 80 minutes to fulfilment!

8: No charity for the YMCA. Harpenden 18 Huddersfield YMCA 14

Huddersfield, much fancied to take the trophy, prove to be by far the hardest side Harpenden have met to date. Fortunately all the pre-match work put in, finding out as much as possible about the Huddersfield side, pays off. Meticulous preparation for the game, played at neutral Burton-on-Trent, produces a game plan which finally wins the day. Huddersfield are taken on in the forwards, and Harpenden play an unusual tactical game of driving and using the rolling maul, with their talented threequarters coming into the picture only on limited occasions. Fortunately, although the threequarters have a bad day as a unit, the forwards play to their peak. A pulsating and very hard game goes to Harpenden by a dramatic injury time try from Andy McPherson, who, along with skipper Chris Wright and No.8 Dan Phillips, is inspirational. Victory ensures the realisation of a dream – a trip to Twickenham. Many, including Huddersfield, think this game is the real final. It shows Harpenden can adapt to different playing circumstances. They prove to be the better side in spite of the narrow margin of victory.

9: The Final hurdle. Harpenden 34 Crewe and Nantwich 31
Having got so far nothing is going to stop Harpenden winning at the mecca of rugby – even though it takes extra time and a recovery from a 13-point deficit. Without their charismatic captain Chris Wright, who has made it his personal crusade to get the side to Twickenham and has been so cruelly denied by breaking his foot in the last second of the final game to clinch the league title, Harpenden, led from the front by No.8 Dan Phillips, turns on the style to entertain the 2,000 fans who have made the trip to Twickenham with a thrilling game, running out victors after extra time. Although the explosive backs take a lot of credit for the victory, the forwards put in a dogged performance, in which the back row of Dan Phillips, Andy McPherson and Tom Stanford are truly outstanding, to overcome a bigger and stronger opposition pack and give the electric back line plenty of possession.

Crewe and Nantwich with their powerful pack try to keep the game tight throughout. Their tactics pay off initially as they are awarded a penalty in the first five minutes and then achieve a push-over try with their next scrum which is duly converted. They are confident on turning round at half-time 13–3 ahead – Dean Ford having kicked a penalty for Harpenden in a rare foray into the opposition half. However, Harpenden's forwards, defying the theory that size, weight and strength is everything, begin to pressurise the opposition pack and produce a stream of good ball which scrum half Rob Humphrey and fly half Dean Ford are able to feed to the Harpenden backs who, having defended stalwartly throughout, show what brilliant attacking players they are, and literally begin to run the show. Their enterprise is rewarded and they begin to look comfortable at 17–13 ahead with Dean Ford making some good kicks. However, some scrappy play lets Crewe back into the game and they force themselves into a 24–17 lead. Harpenden then run in a try through Dave Talbot (who is fed the ball by replacement prop Andy Kiff – his moment of glory) in extra time and Dean Ford converts in the dying seconds, so forcing extra time. They have come back from the brink yet again, with their spirit and running skills. What excitement. The crowd can hardly contain themselves.

In extra time Harpenden's fitness begin to tell. They then look much the better side and a penalty and a try by Simon Smith, make the game look certain. A last-minute push-over try by Crewe does nothing to stop the celebrations that have already begun. Full back Tony Baxter has a superb game in defence, never faltering under the high ball and joining the electric backs in attack to end up with two tries.

The dream has been achieved! Heaven is Twickenham as winning finalists!

Time to party as the Harpenden players celebrate their place in rugby history.

Strange But True

- Wavell Wakefield, captain of the 1924 England Grand Slam side, honed his tackling skills by chasing pigs on a friend's farm. "Take care not to break their legs and watch out for the sharp hooves," was Wakefield's advice.

- Spare a thought for Frenchman Jean Salut. As he ran up the steps onto the pitch to face Scotland in the 1969 Five Nations, he tripped and broke his ankle. He never played for France again.

- On the subject of carelessness, All Black Howard Joseph had a clear run to the try-line during the 1971 third Test against the British Lions. Glory beckoned but in his desperate attempt to evade Lions, Joseph failed to spot a stray dog that had run onto the pitch. Down he went and the Lions took the match 13–3.

- Rugby has always prided itself on its sociability, but General Maritz of the Transvaal Scouting Corps went a step further during the Boer War of 1899–1902. He arranged a 12 hour truce with the British so the two sides could batter each other on a rugby field instead of a battlefield.

- The King's Cross Steelers are Britain's only exclusively gay rugby team. Founded in 1995, the Steelers are based in London and have over 35 members.

- Scottish winger Ken MacLeod should have been delighted when he received his debut call-up against Wales in 1903. Unfortunately, Ken had to tell the selectors he would be unavailable. His headmaster insisted the 15 year-old concentrate on his studies instead. Ken eventually won the first of 10 caps in 1905.

- The 1980 All Black coach came up with a novel way of improving his side's handling skills prior to the Test against Australia. During training he replaced balls with bricks. New Zealand won the match 26–10.

- A Ugandan match in the late 1970s nearly ended in disaster when the home club decided to throw an impromptu post-match fireworks display. As the cracks echoed through the night, the local militia was mobilised and hundreds of heavily-armed troops arrived at the ground expecting to find a revolution in process.

- Who said the Scots were tight? Jock Weymss played twice for Scotland the season before World War One. On the outbreak of war, Wemyss went off to fight and when he returned was picked for the match against France in 1920. Turning up at the Ground without his rugby socks, he was told he wouldn't be given another pair because he should have kept the first pair safe during the war.

- During a club match in France in 1974 between Villiers les Nancy and Villeneuve, les Nancy were winning 65–3 when the Villeneuve winger intercepted a pass and dashed for the try-line. Unfortunately he ran straight into a snowman erected by the bored Nancy full-back as he waited for some action.

Gavin Mortimer Excerpts taken from "14 men and a hooker" – everything you wanted to know about rugby but were afraid to ask – Heineken Exports humorous guide to the World of rugby – available from October 6th by writing to 14 men and a hooker, Unit Three, Tower Workshop, Riley Road, London, SE1 3DG.

HEINEKEN CUP – Here to stay

BY JOHN KENNEDY

The Heineken Cup is already the northern hemisphere club rugby success story of the century. And it will continue to be so, despite all those 'ifs' rather than 'whens' being bandied about barely a year ago as the fledging European club competition was trying to get its second season off the ground.

Thankfully, 36 years on from the then presidential nominee JFK – John Fitzgerald Kennedy – declaring to the United States voters that 'we stand today on the edge of a new frontier', much the same sort of sentiment struck enough chords in European rugby to win the day.

Because the Heineken Cup is already an unqualified success – although its full impact on this new rugby frontier has only just begun, the surface has merely been scratched.

Nevertheless, almost a third of a million spectators went through the turnstiles to see the 46 matches in the 1996–97 pools, quarter-finals and semi-finals.

Match no. 47 was the final. Ah, the Cardiff Arms Park final. Watched by 41,664 lucky ones who will treasure being able to declare, 'I was there,' there were another estimated 35 million armchair viewers in 86 countries, ranging from Australia to Vietnam, who viewed a priceless gem.

While Brive's thoroughly deserved 28–9 victory over Leicester was the showpiece occasion, the tournament had already been snowballing into something special from the day the opening salvoes were fired in mid-October.

For starters, it provided the first sighting to a wider audience of a certain Sebastien Carrat, the 10.35-seconds-for-the-100-metres sprinter who has now put his name up in dazzling Euro lights – tenfold, to be exact.

He started the tournament with four tries against Neath and finished it with two against the Leicester Tigers. In between there were another four, including a 'special' against Harlequins. Without the Heineken Cup the winger's talents could have remained tucked away in Central France – with the Heineken Cup he has become a European rugby household name.

Carrat was followed home in the try chart by Cardiff's Robert Howley and Ugo Mola of Dax with half a dozen each, the latter's clubmate Richard Dourthe hanging on to the top points-scoring spot with his 82, four ahead of Christophe Lamaison.

And, like Carrat, his Brive teammate Gregory Kacala, the barn-storming 27-times-capped Polish international flanker from Gdansk who made huge

Sebastian Carrat outpaces Austin Healey to the line to score Brive's fourth try and his second against Leicester in the final at Cardiff – Carrat was one of the sensations of the tournament.

dents in every opposing side he came up against, is another who can thank the tournament for upping his value by adding a nought or two.

What's more, he impressed Cardiff so much in their semi-final defeat that the Arms Park club and Welsh Cup holders were the ones to finally prize him away from France and get his signature on a three-year contract.

But it was on the collective club front that the Euro game really took off. Where there had been familiarity there was freshness, where there had been comfort zones there were genuine challenges.

'The Heineken Cup will only get bigger,' said Nick Farr-Jones, Australia's 1991 World Cup-winning captain who gave Brive a hand in their tournament preparations. 'It is a tremendously important competition because the northern hemisphere has to make sure it doesn't fall further behind the south.'

Bob Dwyer, who masterminded that Wallabies '91 World Cup triumph for Farr-Jones and Co. and is now the Leicester director of rugby, added, 'The Heineken Cup is a great competition and it will only get better. The standard of performance in the final was outstanding.'

However, once the 1996–97 business was done and dusted, all the chatter at the clubs, provinces and districts from the seven countries involved – England, Ireland, Scotland, Wales, France, Italy and Romania – was about qualifying for the 1997–98 tournament, turning their attentions to domestic issues and ensuring they made their home marks and with that the Euro stage.

Lawrence Dallaglio's Wasps emerged as top dogs from the Courage League to earn the right to be the England standard bearers in Europe in 1997–98 and they, along with Bath, NEC Harlequins and Leicester, will be all the better prepared this time after their belated entry into the tournament.

Bath in particular regarded last season as a major Euro disappointment, losing to Pontypridd and Cardiff on their two ventures across the Severn, and although they did reach the quarter-finals, they will be desperate for a better showing this time.

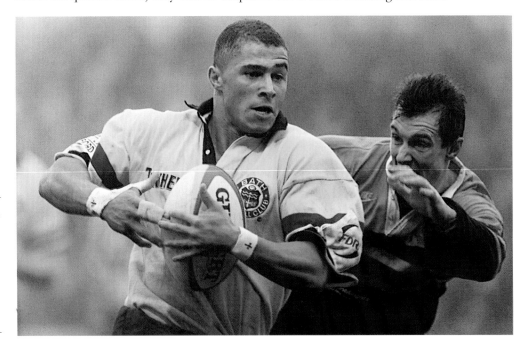

Jason Robinson tries to round Cardiff scrum half Rob Howley in the game which saw Bath depart the competition at the quarter-final stage.

Meanwhile, with a first Welsh National League title under their belts, Pontypridd will go into the tournament with confidence sky high and, in fly half Neil Jenkins, they have one the world's greatest goal kickers to take advantage of any opposition lapses.

Swansea, under John Plumtree, their new director of coaching, failed to qualify for last season's event, but having been there before in 1995, they know what to expect from the European challenge.

There is no change in either the Irish challenge – Munster, Leinster and Ulster qualifying again – or in the Italian representation in the shape of Benneton Treviso and Milan, though Treviso have stopped Milan's recent domination of their domestic championship. Glasgow are the new boys from Scotland, joining Caledonia and Scottish Borders.

However, the challenge for all those is just how they can crack the French stranglehold on both the Heineken Cup and the second-tier European Conference. Seven of the last eight in the latter were Gallic while France supplied two of the Heineken Cup semi-finalists before, a year on, Alain Penaud of Brive followed Emile Ntamack of Toulouse up the same Arms Park steps to claim the ultimate prize.

Toulouse certainly know how to rise to the occasion, turning what was for them a relatively mediocre season into triumph when they won the French title for a remarkable fourth straight year.

Bourgoin were the surprise package, restricting Toulouse to a narrow 12–6 championship final victory at Parc des Princes, with Pau qualifying as the Challenge Du Manoir winners and Brive as the defending cup holders, the only query over the latter this time coming in the shape of how they will make up for the huge loss of Kacala.

What is not in doubt collectively, however, is that the belated introduction of English and Scottish teams added a new profile and a new edge to the competition, though the Scots disappointed in managing only one win from their 12 fixtures, Scottish Borders beating Llanelli 24–16.

Benetton Treviso notched up the first and, so far, only Italian success in the competition, winning 43–23 in Edinburgh, with Leicester, Bath, Harlequins and Wasps helping to make England the most successful country at the end of the pools stage.

Between them they won 12 out of their 16 fixtures, followed by France (11 out of 16), Wales (10 out of 16), Ireland (five out of 12), Italy (one out of eight) and Scotland (one out of 12).

Leicester were the only ones to win on French soil, a stunning 19–14 away-day-to-savour at Pau, as the 40 pool matches produced 248 tries at an average of 6.2 per match. As the tournament headed for the knock-out stages, Cardiff produced a titanic display to account for Bath 22–19, Toulouse won the 'Battle of France', 26–18 winners at Dax, while Leicester and Brive made home advantage count for the visits of Harlequins and Llanelli.

With television at last on board across the board, the semi-finals on the first weekend of January reached parts not previously reached before – Leicester's home tie with Toulouse attracted a BBC *Grandstand* audience of 4.1 million, with a peak of 5.8 million, as the Tigers streamrolled the French champions to a 37–11 defeat in front of a Welford Road capacity crowd of 16,300.

The Sunday special at Parc Municipal des Sports also pulled them in through the turnstiles – but only after a monumental salvage effort by the

Austin Healey and Graham Rowntree celebrate the try which saw the Tigers through to the final with an impressivre victory over Toulouse in front of a capacity Welford Road crowd.

home club after a blizzard threatened to force the game to be postponed. Sixty volunteers, working throughout the night, followed by 70 servicemen at the break of dawn, between them shifted 200,000 tonnes of snow and 25 tonnes of hay to reveal an impeccable playing surface. That, however, was as good as it got for Cardiff. Brive shut them out totally – in hindsight giving Leicester a taste of what was to come at the neutral Arms Park venue in the pulsating climax.

French participation ensured a carnival atmosphere with the release of thousands of balloons in the teams' colours and the rival bands thundering out their support creating something really special.

If that produced a marvellous buzz, the action itself was even better ... providing you weren't a Tigers fan. Brive went off like a rocket and although Christophe Lamaison had a rare off day with the boot, they did the job with the ball in hand.

Full back Sebastien Viars got the first of their four tries after just six minutes, right wing Gerald Fabre the next and then that man Carrat wrapped it up in style with the final two in a thumping victory.

The Brive players huddle in celebration after the final whistle. Their victory over Leicester in the final continued the French monopoly of the competition.

'If there are still doubters as to the value and quality of the Heineken Cup, they should leave the room now,' Paul Ackford wrote in the *Sunday Telegraph*. 'It was sensational. If only rugby could always be this wonderful, this was a staggering match, a celebration of rugby at its passionate, primeval best.'

That clearly leaves no doubt of the impact that the 1996–97 tournament in general, and the final in particular, has made on the former Lions and England second-row forward – that it is a competition that has taken the northern hemisphere club game well and truly across the divide and into that new frontier. Now the stage is set to take that process another giant step forward.

The 20 teams who have qualified for the 1997–98 tournament are:

England: Wasps, Bath, NEC Harlequins, Leicester.
France: Toulouse, Bourgoin, Brive, Pau
Ireland: Munster, Leinster, Ulster
Italy: Benetton Treviso, Milan
Scotland: Caledonia, Glasgow, Scottish Borders
Wales: Pontypridd, Swansea

THE HEINEKEN CUP 1996-97 REVIEW

Pool A

Pontypridd 28 Treviso 22; Bath 55 Edinburgh 26; Pontypridd 32 Edinburgh 10; Dax 34 Treviso 14; Pontypridd 16 Bath 6; Dax 69 Edinburgh 12; Bath 25 Dax 16; Treviso 43 Edinburgh 23; Dax 22 Pontypridd 18; Bath 50 Treviso 27.

Pool B

Pau 85 Scottish Borders 28; Llanelli 34 Leinster 17; Scottish Borders 24 Llanelli 16; Llanelli 31 Pau 15; Leicester 43 Scottish Borders 3; Leicester 27 Leinster 10; Leicester 19 Pau 14; Leinster 34 Scottish Borders 25; Leinster 25 Pau 23; Leicester 25 Llanelli 16.

Pool C

Brive 34 Neath 19; Ulster 41 Caledonia 34; Neath 27 Caledonia 18; Harlequins 21 Ulster 15; Harlequins 44 Neath 22; Brive 32 Caledonia 30; Brive 23 Harlequins 10; Neath 15 Ulster 13; Brive 17 Ulster 6; Harlequins 56 Caledonia 36.

Pool D

Munster 23 Milan 5; Cardiff 26 Wasps 24; Cardiff 48 Munster 18; Toulouse 44 Milan 26; Munster 49 Wasps 22; Toulouse 36 Cardiff 20; Wasps 77 Toulouse 17; Cardiff 41 Milan 19; Toulouse 60 Minster 19; Wasps 33 Milan 23.

Quarter-finals

Cardiff 22 Bath 19; Toulouse 26 Dax 18; Leicester 23 Harlequins 13; Brive 35 Llanelli 14.

Semi-finals

Leicester 37 Toulouse 11; Brive 26 Cardiff 13.

Heineken Cup final

Brive 28 Leicester 9
Brive: *Tries* S Carrat (2), S Viars, G Fabre; *Conversion* C Lamaison; *Penalty goal* C Lamaison; *Drop goal* C Lamaison.
Leicester: *Penalty goals* J Liley (3)

Captain Alain Penaud raises the Heineken Cup to the hordes of Brive supporters who had made the journey to Cardiff.

Always ahead of the pack...

SEREVI'S SANYO SUCCESS

BY NIGEL STARMER-SMITH

Some players best ride the rugby pitch like Colossi, dominating the action by their sheer physical presence. One can think back to Colin Meads and Willie John McBride, Ian Kirkpatrick or Warrick Fay, or in the contemporary international scene, to players such as Jonah Lomu or Olivier Merle. But a significant part of the enduring appeal of rugby is that vastness is not pre-requisite for a player in the way that success in top-flight basketball demands pre-eminence in tallness. In the 15-a-side game small men can win.

I mention this not just because I have a natural sympathy for those lacking in height, but because it was a little man who made the visit to Twickenham on 24 May for the Sanyo Challenge Cup more than worth the effort. I will admit to having been amongst those sceptics who thought that this end-of-season exhibition was a 'game too far'. With attention already focused on the Lions in South Africa, cup and league finals in all the Home Counties already played out, and those not involved in touring relishing a break from the game, what purpose did this celebration serve? Furthermore, whilst leading world players were happy to enjoy a visit to Twickenham, suitably rewarded in cash and kind, the privilege of facing a star-studded World XV, captained by Philippe Sella, was problematic for Courage League champions, Wasps shorn of their title-winning complement by the absence of Lawrance Dallaglio, Chris Sheasby, Andy Gomarsall, Alex King and Nick Greenstock on Lions or England duty. Bolstered by the presence of 'honorary Wasp', former Wales captain Mike Hall, there was however, no lack of incentive for the Wasps 'understudies': a chance to play at Twickenham – many for the

Peter Scrivener drives forward as Wasps hold their own against the World XV.

first time; the opportunity to compete with top internationals from nine nations; and not least, an occasion on which to display their talents amongst the best. For such as the restructured Wasps back row of Buster White, Peter Scrivener and Matt Greenwood, young prop forwards Will Green and Adam Black, and 20-year-old scrum half Martyn Wood, it was a chance well taken as reputations were happily enhanced. But back to the 'star of the show' – no Colossus he, but more a puckish, waif-like figure – Waisale Serevi of Fiji.

Shortly before kick-off Leicester coach Bob Dwyer, appointed to direct affairs for the Word XV on the field, mentioned to me that he was well-nigh

Bryan Redpath spins the ball out to release the World XV'x multi-talented back division.

certain that Serevi and fellow Fijian Marika Vunibaka would be joining the Tigers for the 1997–98 season – but please don't announce it in the commentary. It was to be made public on the following Monday. How he must have preened inwardly as his two new recruits stole the show. The World XV – with 666 caps between them – had no mean platform up front off which to play: a Springbok front row of Balie Swart, James Dalton and Dawie Theron; another South African Hannes Strydom alongside Olivier Roumat behind; and a back-row trio for any rugby enthusiast to savour in Willie Ofahengaue, Jamie Joseph and François Pienaar – not to mention Jean-Michel Gonzalez, Fritz van Heerden and Nick Popplewell in reserve! No wonder there was to be no shortage of possession for the 20,000 or so to see put to good use by Graeme Bachop, David Campese, Eric Rush, 'will-o-the-wisp' Argentinian Lisandra Arbiju, Sebastian Viars, Bryan Redpath, Japan's Yoshihito Yoshida, together with Sella and the two Fijians in an irresistible combination. But, thankfully, this was no Sunday afternoon charity runabout – Wasps ensured that the game was played at full throttle, bringing out the best from the resourceful team of all the talents.

Above all here was a rare chance to see the world's greatest-ever exponent of the seven-a-side art – most recently having led Fiji to the world title in Hong Kong – playing the 15-a-side game. With 7s the national game of Fiji and their inability to get to grips with the art of forward play thwarting their attempts to become a world power in the full game (they even failed to qualify for the World Cup finals in 1995), Serevi has seldom had the opportunity to express his talents fully on the international circuit. But now, with ball in hand, he taunted, mesmerised, light of foot and deft of hand, throwing outrageous dummies, gliding through gaps, accelerating silkily into space to offload the scoring pass or run it in himself for the try. Three of the Word XVs eight tries came from the 29-year-old maestro himself, whilst the formidable Vunibaka – another star of the world champion 7s team with a back-row forward's physique and the running skills of a thoroughbred sprinter – left his indelible mark on proceedings with two wonderful scoring runs.

But Wasps certainly had their say on their hard-earned day – the reward for a popular league-season triumph. Gareth Rees (stand-in captain for Dallaglio) hot-foot back from Hong Kong where he had been representing Canada in the World Cup 7s was his masterly controlling self – as befits a man who has already represented his country in all three World Cups. The Scottish pair of Andy Reed and Damien Cronin ensured a good contest in the line out with some great constructive and destructive play from the back row. Fellow Scot Kenny Logan added weight to the argument that he was unlucky not to make the Lions tour as wing threequarter. He scored two fine tries, while Shane Roiser and a deserving 'Buster' White added two more late in the day to make the 31–52 final scoreline more than just respectable.

Perhaps after all there didn't need to be a specific meaning to the occasion. The pleasure provided for the vociferous crowd was reason enough to justify the event – world-class players in a real game displaying real talent was satisfying. The Wasps contingent made them play hard to win, and as Prince Michael of Kent presented the Sanyo Challenge Cup to the ageless Sella, we could all reflect – even we sceptic journalists – on an afternoon of rugby fun. But, oh, what about Waisale!

The star of the show, Waisale Serevi, conjures up more magic to thrill the Twickenham crowd.

...another great conversion

Coopers & Lybrand is delighted to have assisted the Scottish Rugby Union with their successful £36.75 million issue of debentures and the conversion of Murrayfield into a world class rugby stadium.

Solutions for Business

- business assurance ○ business recovery and insolvency
- corporate finance ○ management consulting
- tax and human resource advice

PREVIEW OF THE SEASON 1997–98

THE FIVE NATIONS CHAMPIONSHIP

BY BILL McLAREN

Things are looking up in the Five Nations championship – and they should look up even further during the 1998 series if the trend set in the previous season provides the blue print.

Of course in the minds of most folk, the Five Nations has become an annual duel between England and France for the top honour with the Celtic nations battling away on more slender resources trying both to keep their heads above water and to steer clear of a whitewash. Not only that, but the Five Nations cuts little ice with the heavyweights of the southern hemisphere who regard the European game as a pale offshoot of their own sensationally spectacular style of play.

Nonetheless the Five Nations remains the jewel in the European crown, and still stimulates huge interest and mighty endeavour in the five countries involved. One wonders, too, how long the improving Italians can be kept out of the championship – especially if you consider their 40–32 win over France in Grenoble. If Italy had been in the 1997 championship, the final placings, on the basis of their results against the other Five Nations sides, would have been : England 8 points, France 8, Wales 4, Italy 4, Scotland 4, Ireland 2.

There were signs in the championship last season that the new age of professionalism with its higher levels of fitness and skills and a more improved degree of teamwork, was producing an altogether higher brand of performance, both individual and collective, and this was mirrored in the increased number of tries scored. There is much more to 80 minutes of cap-international play than try-scoring – as the British Lions showed in their second Test against the Springboks – but there is no doubt that it is the scoring of tries that brings an audience to its feet with a sharp intake of breath. In the ten games of the 1996 Five Nations 355 points, including 30 tries, were scored. In last season's series the number of points had risen to 511 and tries to 53. Considering that in 1993 the number of tries scored was just 20, it just goes to show how much the Five Nations game has sprung to life.

The reasons are not hard to find. Full-time players, contracted to their clubs, districts and unions, are fitter and stronger and, because they train together more often, their skill levels and intuitive teamwork are of a higher grade. Also the effect of the Super 12 series in the southern hemisphere has been a factor. They have taken the game to a new level, with longer spells of continuous action, with the ball being recycled more quickly and more often, and with slick ball transference and support running that has spawned a shoal of dramatic scores. The crowds have loved it, and so, too, have those in the northern hemisphere who have been lucky enough to view it on their television screens. There is little doubt that the influence of the southern hemisphere style has been keenly felt in the Five Nations and there is every reason to hope that there will be even more exciting, flowing rugby in the 1998 campaign.

One other hopeful sign is that the 39 British Lions who took part in some or all of the recent tour to South Africa will have returned to their clubs, districts and international squads having been part of an effort by the Lions to embrace a flowing 15-man game. Ian McGeechan, the Lions' coach, clearly aimed those Lions towards fluency of action as the best means of defeating the Springboks, but also wanted to show the southern hemisphere that they have no monopoly on quality, total rugby. Hopefully those Lions will want to continue that process with their squads at each grade to the eventual benefit of style in the Five Nations.

England should gain most advantage having had 23 Englishmen on that tour. They will have returned with new ideas on how to prepare for playing in an attractive style. One need only recall the glorious movement leading to Lawrence Dallagio's try against Natal to recognise the type of ball transference that can so enliven the action in the modern game – even allowing for the tightness of modern defensive marking. When one remembers, too, the amount of punting in recent Five Nations campaigns it was note-worthy that those Lions had made up their minds not to concede ball to the opposition through punting, but to maintain possession by playing with ball in hand. It made for much richer entertainment. Hopefully this will be carried through to the 1998 Five Nations championship.

Tim Stimpson dives over the line to score in England's impressive win over Wales in Cardiff. Stimpson will be hoping to fend off intense competition for his place in the forthcoming season.

England's problem this time round (and not for the first time) will be who to leave out. One example lies in the claims of rival full backs Tim Stimpson (Newcastle), Jon Callard (Bath), Nick Beal (Northampton) and John Mallinder (Sale). Into the wing equation comes John Bentley (Newcastle) who scored the try of the Lions' tour with a stunning combination of pace and swerve over 70 metres against the Gauteng Lions. If there was one setback for England emanating from the Lions' tour it was the inclusion of seven English forwards in the pack who were embarrassingly outscrummaged by Western

Province. But England, as always, will be able to field a big, ball-winning, driving pack with a formidable loose forward combination, although the controversy over whether to play Neil Back (Leicester) or Richard Hill (Saracens) at open side is bound to continue.

England arguably made the biggest strides towards a more entertaining style in as much as they scored only three tries in winning the 1996 Five Nations title but amassed 15 tries last season in an attractive mix of drive and speed.

It had to be expected that France would seek to mould their flamboyant style on the

Abdelatif Benazzi raises the Five Nations trophy aloft (right) as the French team celebrate in front of their home crowd after defeating Scotland to claim their first Grand Slam since 1988.

southern hemisphere method, especially as their coaches Jean-Claude Skrela and Pierre Villepreux are renowned for embracing a risk factor in their exciting strategy. France will defend their 1996–97 Grand Slam with all their characteristic instinctive adventurism and flair. Even though they lost both Tests to the Wallabies on their summer tour, 29–15 and 26–19, their pack still looked heavy and formidable and they are still top dogs at hitting on the break. France last season unearthed another new midfield talent in Brive's Christophe Lamaison who scored 26 points in two internationals, 18 of them in the 23–20 victory over England at Twickenham. There was, too, a new dynamic flanker in Olivier Magne who scored a great try against Scotland and, of course, France achieved a Grand Slam without the services of Emile Ntamack, Thomas Castaignède, Philippe Saint-André, who has captained France 29 times, Olivier Roumat and Christian

Califano. No doubt Skrela and Villepreux will be hoping to recapture the breathtaking form of their 47–20 defeat of Scotland that clinched the Grand Slam in Paris on 15 March.

Wales hoped last season that their returned Rugby League stalwarts – Scott Gibbs, Allan Bateman, Scott Quinnell and David Young – would bring about the revival in their fortunes for which their demanding support yearn, but a 34–19 win at Murrayfield was their only Five Nations victory. Perhaps this season will see the Rugby League influence at its strongest, but allied to that is the need to put together a strong platform up front so that their potentially gifted backs will have the kind of ammunition that will enable them to display traditional Welsh skill, flair and *hwyl*. Wales, however, will be at some disadvantage since their beloved National Stadium is currently receiving a £114 million reconstruction in time for the 1999 Rugby World Cup. The Welsh players may not respond as well at Wembley without that special Cardiff *hwyl*. Their six-game July tour of North America, with Gwyn Jones of Cardiff as captain and with two Tests against Canada and one against the United States, will have provided helpful evidence of the potential of several players capable of knocking on the international door. To make matters worse, they open their championship campaign at Twickenham on 21 February where they haven't won since 1988.

Olivier Merle (above) celebrates the French win at Twickenham. Whilst many believe this year's Five Nations will be between France and England, Wales will be hoping for a major contribution from their Rugby League contingent – Scott Quinnell (left), Scott Gibbs, Allan Bateman and David Young.

No doubt Ireland will prove as unpredictable as ever, but the effect of Brian Ashton's coaching methods should be more influential in this his second season. He will have Lions' lore from Ireland's four in South Africa – Paul Wallace, Keith Wood, Jeremy Davidson and Eric Miller – to reinforce his own input and even though the Irish Development Squad, captained by Gary Halpin, had a hard row to hoe in their summer tour of New Zealand, they will have returned wiser and more conversant with the commitments required to match the heavyweights in the international game.

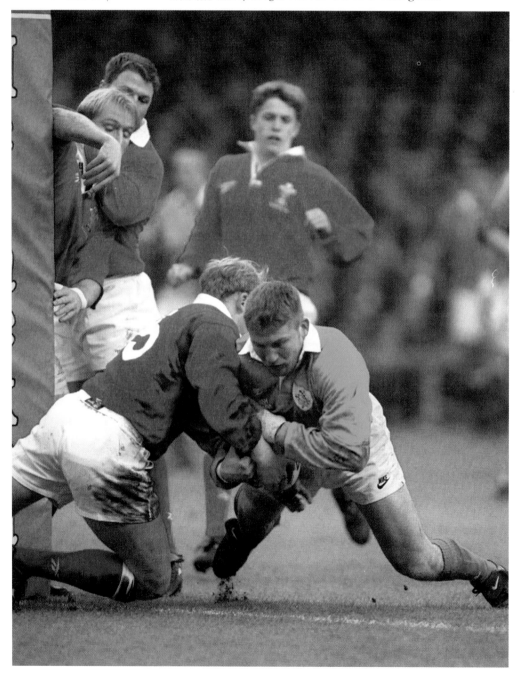

Jonathan Bell dives between the posts during Ireland's victory against Wales at Cardiff. Their chances for the 1998 championship remain as hard to predict as ever.

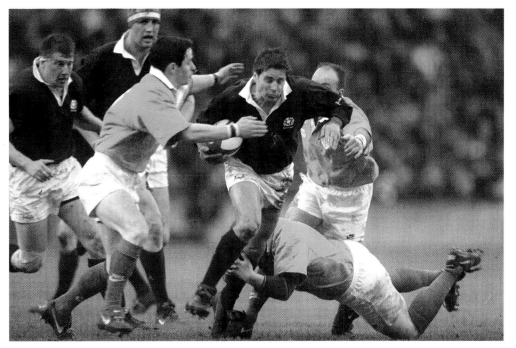

Scotland, however, could be the main beneficiaries of the summer tours for not only did they have five in the Lions' party in South Africa – Gregor Townsend, Alan Tait, Tom Smith, Doddie Weir and Rob Wainwright, plus Tony Stanger as a late replacement – they also toured Zimbabwe and South Africa in June and July with a tough six-game programme that started with a 55–10 win over Zimbabwe and an unexpected 33–22 win over the Blue Bulls, Northern Transvaal. They lost Craig Chalmers, Rowen Shepherd and Ian Smith early through injury, but unearthed some rare prospects in locks Andrew Lucking (Currie) and Scott Murray (Bedford), a 20-year-old centre with the build and approach of a Scott Gibbs in the Watsonian Jamie Mayer, a quicksilver midfield player in Cameron Murray (Hawick) and the Watsonians stand off Duncan Hodge, capped as a replacement for Craig Chalmers in the France v Scotland game in March.

Scotland also broke new ground by sending a 20-strong party of younger players, called the Silver Thistles, to play in New Zealand during the summer. The players were to be based in twos at clubs in the North Island, to be given a taste of New Zealand club play, whilst also playing four games against provincial development opposition. There was only one capped player in the squad in front-five forward Alan Watt of Currie. Most of all, Scotland will be hoping that Doddie Weir will be completely restored after the shocking injury that put him out of the Lions' tour.

All of which, when coupled with the visit to the UK of all three southern hemisphere giants during the autumn should make for a fascinating Five Nations series which opens on 7 February with France v England and Ireland v Scotland. For the first time two internationals will be played on Sunday – Scotland v England on 22 March and Wales v France on 5 April.

Heavy betting no doubt will favour that the France v England confrontation in the new Paris stadium on 7 February will be the likely championship decider. Perhaps so. Hopefully, the Celts will be able to mount a powerful challenge in a memorable campaign. And 55 tries would go down pretty well too!

Meet David.

David's investments used to be (un)managed by David, until he asked for some expert help.

David has spent a lifetime acquiring shares and opening savings accounts, and would be the first to describe his portfolio as "a bit of a mixed bag, to be honest." Which is why David asked about Midland Private Banking, a service that gives each of its customers a dedicated manager to manage their portfolio of stocks and shares. The managers can offer independent advice on pensions, trusts, wills and investments; they will handle all the administration; they can even do your tax returns. If – like David – you don't pay enough attention to your finances and would like to have someone who does, and you've got savings and investments of over one hundred thousand pounds call 0800 180 180 for a brochure.

Midland Private Banking

Member HSBC *Group*

He called
0800 180 180
for a brochure.

Pick up the phone,

or cut the coupon.

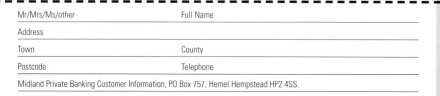

Mr/Mrs/Ms/other	Full Name
Address	
Town	County
Postcode	Telephone

Midland Private Banking Customer Information, PO Box 757, Hemel Hempstead HP2 4SS.

KEY PLAYERS 1997–98

BY IAN ROBERTSON

ENGLAND

AUSTIN HEALEY

RICHARD HILL

At the start of last season, it seemed as if the battle to be England's scrum half would be between Kyran Bracken, Matt Dawson and Andy Gomersall. However, the Leicester scrum half Austin Healey had an outstanding year at club level and forced his way into the England side as first choice for the last international against Wales, having won his first cap as a replacement against Ireland. He played so well in that game that he was selected for the British Lions tour to South Africa. He began his senior career on the wing for Orrell at a time when the club scrum half was Dewi Morris. When Morris retired, Healey switched from wing to scrum half and he then switched from Orrell to Leicester. His great strength is his tremendous speed and he has made his reputation with a series of devastating breaks from rucks and mauls as well as from set-pieces. His service was not of international standard when he joined Leicester, but this aspect of his game has steadily improved and with the experience of the Lions tour behind him, he can look forward with confidence to playing a full part this season in England's new exciting brand of dynamic rugby.

In the space of one short season Richard Hill has made a terrific impact on the England team and the new dynamic style of English play. In the previous couple of seasons England had gone for three big, strong, tall forwards in the back row without selecting a genuine open-side flanker. They had picked from a selection of No.8s including Dean Richards, Ben Clarke, Lawrence Dallaglio, Tim Rodber and Steve Ojomoh. Last season, England followed the example of South Africa, New Zealand and Australia and went for a specialist open side. Richard Hill made a huge difference with his speed to the breakdown and his creative play in the open. He has good hands and with his insight into the game is a very good support player as well as a formidable tackler. He has had a distinguished representative career with England having played at schoolboy, Colts and Student level before playing for England 'A' and then the full England side in the Calcutta Cup match in 1997. He scored a try against Scotland and won selection for the British Lions.

FRANCE

CHRISTOPHE LAMAISON

ABDELATIF BENAZZI

The French have produced quite a few multi-talented backs in the last ten years and the latest to be given potential superstar status is Christophe Lamaison. He began his senior club career with Bayonne as a wing but he soon became equally effective at centre and at full back before switching to fly half. He is a beautifully balanced runner with impressive acceleration and has the ability to beat a defence even in a confined space. Indeed, at the RFU Awards dinner in May 1997, he was presented with a special award by the chief executive of Save & Prosper Peter Roney as the player who produced the outstanding performance in the Five Nations championship against England. He not only scored one try, one dropped goal, two conversions and two penalties in this match to help France win, but he was a threat to England all afternoon. In 1994, he was brought into the French squad for the international against New Zealand but he had to wait another two years before winning his first cap against South Africa when he came on as a replacement in Bordeaux. He began 1997 in a blaze of glory producing an inspirational display for Brive against Leicester in the Heineken Cup final.

Right through the 1990s France have begun almost every season as favourites to win the Five Nations championship but they have been perennial under-achievers. It was not until 1997 that they enjoyed their fifth Grand Slam ever and their first since 1987. One of the main reasons for their change of fortune has been the appointment of Abdelatif Benazzi as their new captain. Not only is he just about the best back-row forward in world rugby, he has been a great captain, imposing his personality on the team and their style of rugby. He has brought much-needed discipline and control to the French side – qualities that have been sadly lacking in recent years. Born in Morocco, he settled in France in 1988 and two years later he won his first cap for France against Australia. He made a little piece of history when he was sent off early in the first half of that match but he learned his lesson and nowadays not only does he have his priorities right he has instilled these priorities in the rest of his side. Outstanding in the loose and at the back of the line out, he is equally good with the ball in his hands going forward or mustering his troops in defence. With Benazzi in command, France will be favourites for the Grand Slam yet again.

IRELAND

ERIC MILLER

JEREMY DAVIDSON

The Irish pack has been regalvanised in 1997 with the inclusion of Eric Miller at No.8. He made a dramatic impact in his first season of international rugby in the Five Nations championship and he could well became as important to Irish rugby as Dean Richards was for the best part of a decade for English rugby. He moved from Ireland to join Leicester two years ago and spent his early days in English first division club rugby understudying Dean Richards. Of much the same build he had many similar characteristics to 'Deano' and it is highly likely the Irish will build their whole forward effort around him He has already become the apex of their forward thrust and looks set for a very long run in the Irish side. He has safe hands, reads the game well and is also outstanding in defence. By the end of last season, he had displaced Richards in the Leicester side and benefited greatly from playing in such a good club pack, surrounded by people of the highest quality like Rowntree, Cockerill, Johnson and Back. He won his first cap against Italy and then went on to play in the Five Nations before heading off to South Africa with the British Lions. He looks like being a real force for some time to come.

One of Ireland's problem areas in recent seasons has been their inability to win their fair share of good, clean line-out possession, but that has all changed in the past two seasons with the selection of Jeremy Davidson in the back row in 1996 and at lock in 1997. He first sprang to prominence at schoolboy representative level and quickly developed at senior level with Dungannon. Playing mostly in the back row he was chosen to tour Australia with the full Irish squad in 1994 at the age of 20 and he played in four of the eight tour matches. He won his first full cap against Fiji in 1995 and the following year he played right through the Five Nations championship. At 6ft 6ins and 18 stones he is in the enviable position of having the height and weight of a second-row forward but also the speed and creativity of a back-row forward. He moved from Dungannon to London Irish last season and in the more competitive structure of English club rugby he has developed and improved quite dramatically. He is now firmly established in the Ireland side and fully deserved his selection for the British Lions.

SCOTLAND

DODDIE WEIR

GREGOR TOWNSEND

Having played for Scotland right through the 1990s, Doddie Weir has benefited from his versatility being equally effective at lock forward or in the back row and is well on his way to winning 50 caps for his country. He won his first cap at the age of 20 in 1990 against Argentina and went on to play half-a-dozen matches in the World Cup in 1991. At 6ft 7ins and 17 stones he is big enough and heavy enough to play in the second row and with the distinct advantage of being a natural ball-player he is a first-class line-out expert. But he is also quick around the field and considering what a good 7s player he is, it is no wonder he is also an outstanding back row in the 15-a-side game. He was a key member of the Melrose team which won the Scottish club championship four times between 1990 and 1994 but two years ago he left Melrose for Newcastle. He was one of the few major successes in a disappointing season for Scotland in 1997 and certainly deserved his selection for the British Lions. He currently holds the unique record of scoring two tries for Scotland in the same match against New Zealand in the 1995 World Cup and as long as he recovers fully from the injury he sustained on the Lions, tour he looks sure to continue to be a key player for Scotland through to the next World Cup.

Few players have burst on to the international scene with more potential or as dramatically than Gregor Townsend did in 1994, although it should be pointed out he won his first cap at the age of 19 when he came on as a replacement against England. He is one of the most exciting runners in the northern hemisphere and not only does he have an eye for the gap, he has blistering acceleration to go with it. His main problem is the fact that he has been a victim of his own versatility because of his 25 caps for Scotland, he has played almost as many games in the centre as he has at fly half. Most people believe that fly half is his best position but, unfortunately, with his club side Northampton he is forced to play the majority of his matches in the centre, as Paul Grayson also plays for Northampton. This had a detrimental effect on his play in 1997 and he did not recapture the brilliant form he showed in his first three years of international rugby. But the talent and the potential remain and there is no doubt that Townsend at his best raises the spirit and the morale of the whole Scottish squad.

WALES

NEIL JENKINS

SCOTT GIBBS

At the comparatively young age of 26, Neil Jenkins has already joined that élite group of players who have won 50 caps for Wales and, barring injury, it looks pretty certain that by the next World Cup, he and Ieuan Evans will be the only Welsh internationals with over 60 caps. This much understated player has two records which will not be broken for a long time to come. He is the most capped Welsh fly half in history with a total of 35 which beats Cliff Morgan's tally of 29 and he has scored the most points for Wales (534 points). That remarkable record is the fourth highest in world rugby behind Michael Lynagh, Gavin Hastings and Grant Fox. While fly half is generally considered his best position, he has also won eight caps in the centre and seven at full back. He is much more than just a superb kicker of the ball. He has excellent hands, he is deceptively quick off his mark and he can vary the game depending on the circumstances. There is no fly half better equipped to play to his forwards, but he can unleash a threequarter line with the best of them and he has now proved he can also take on the role of the running full back. In the long term he is likely to revert to fly half, but in either position he will be a crucial member of the Welsh team through to the 1999 World Cup.

The new professional era has had immediate beneficial effects for Wales. In the time it takes to make a few phone calls, a few world-class rugby players were persuaded to switch back to Rugby Union from the game of Rugby League which they joined in the preceding half-a-dozen years. Back into the Rugby Union fold came David Young, Scott Quinnell, Jonathan Davies, Allan Bateman and Scott Gibbs. Welsh rugby could suddenly look to the future with real optimism and they now have the makings of a very good back division. With the brilliant Howley at scrum half to control the pace and direction of the game, the Welsh can now also rely on Scott Gibbs to make all the right decisions in midfield. He won the first of his 28 caps against England in 1991 and then played right through to the end of the 1993 Five Nations adding a British Lions tour to New Zealand in 1993 where he displaced Will Carling in the Test team. When he signed for Rugby League he left a big gap in the Welsh side, but he has returned a stronger, better player. His basic skills are as good as ever, but even though he is now a more robust, physical centre he has still retained all his speed and his cutting edge. His defence is devastating. He will be a real force in the Welsh centre for the foreseeable future.

succeed where competition is fierce

THE
PILKINGTON
CUP

In highly competitive international markets, Pilkington stays ahead manufacturing and marketing flat and safety glass products in over 20 countries around the globe.

PILKINGTON

SPONSOR OF THE RFU CLUB KNOCKOUT COMPETITION

THE CLUB SCENE

ENGLAND – Wasps take top honours

BY BILL MITCHELL

The domestic game in England has become a series of contradictions. On the one hand it seems impossible for those who inhabit the Twickenham offices to agree with each other on anything at the same time, worse still, they make their mutual antipathies as public as they can. On the other hand, the game in this country has reached an all-time high in terms of entertainment value.

The huge rise in playing standards at clubs would be excellent news were it not for the fact that a price has to be paid for such enjoyment. That price is the presence of many of the world's top players – Michael Lynagh, François Pienaar, Joel Stransky, Laurent Cabannes, Thierry Lacroix to name but a few – and they will be joined by many more next season as clubs are forced to look to overseas talent to maintain their position at the top of the game.

These people cost money, as do most of the top domestic players, and the clubs are in danger of bankrupting themselves if the trend continues. The game's 'sugar daddies' cannot be guaranteed to foot the bills for ever and any leading club which does not recognise this danger is guilty of extreme stupidity.

Of course, mergers with leading soccer clubs have their advantages, but how long will the game's round ball partners tolerate the wear and tear on their pitches from teams which only rarely draw large crowds. Wasps now operate from Queen's Park Rangers' Loftus Road ground, where their fans are not exactly undercharged for the privilege, and other arrangements are fraught with danger particularly if the soccer clubs decide to demand larger rents to compensate for extra maintenance costs.

One would hope that the rugby clubs have taken all the potential drawbacks into consideration. However, the declared financial state of one of the game's big spenders Harlequins, does not provide any reassurances that top officials are paying too much attention to the obvious dangers. Their expensive team needed to find success, but could only finish third in the league and were beaten Pilkington Cup semi-finalists. As a result of internal differences, their high-profile coach Dick Best departed at the end of the season – and not without acrimony. That he was not the only soccer-style managerial departure suggests that this is the shape of things to come.

The fans in their turn are not being treated too well either. The majority of them cannot obtain tickets for the big games and, in the future, must rely on BSkyB to see England's matches. In an attempt to meet their huge cash requirements, the RFU have been compelled to sacrifice the best interests of fans to cover their own financial shortfalls. Their own protestations that there are no plans for fans to be charged extra for high-profile matches may be true now, but what about the near future? Your guess may be the same as mine.

The English club game, however, was of a very high standard, with the foreign imports, almost without exception, giving of their best. Having said last year that Bath

(Above) The Wasps' players celebrate their Courage League championship. Captain Lawrence Dallaglio and Alex King (right) show off the trophy to their fans.

and Leicester would probably be England's two top clubs, I am not unhappy to report that Wasps comfortably took the Courage League's top honour with Bath second, and Leicester, last season's Pilkington Cup finalists, going one better this time with victory at Twickenham over Sale – a game which possibly signalled the end of the brilliant career of Dean Richards, who made a brief appearance as a replacement.

The final was a sign of the times as the game's two scorers were Joel Stransky, South Africa's 1995 World Cup winner, with three penalties against a single penalty in reply by Sale's Simon Mannix from New Zealand. Both Bath and Wasps had disappeared before the quarter-final stage, Bath at home to Leicester (39–28) and Wasps in a thriller at Saracens (21–17).

Sale's season ended in disappointment. Apart from losing to Leicester in the Pilkington Cup final, they lost the last league match of the season (also against the Tigers) to miss out on the last Heineken Cup spot. They proved, however, that under the coaching expertise of New Zealander John Mitchell they can be

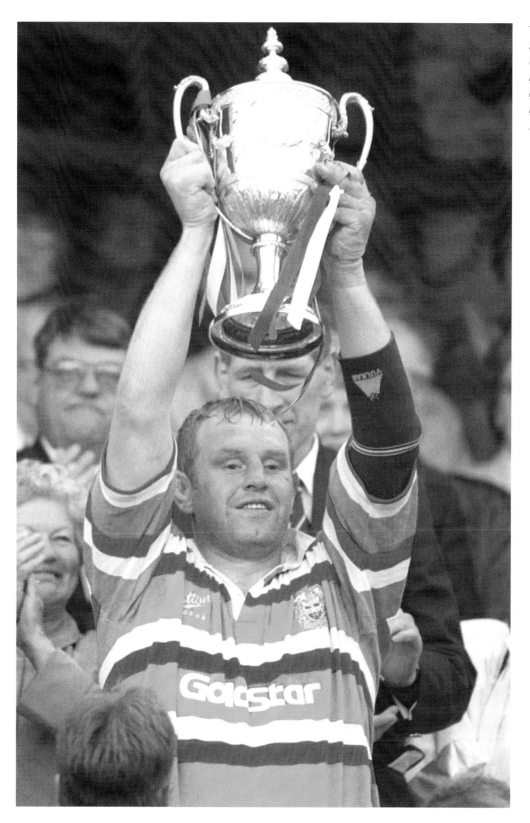

Leicester's Pilkington Cup victory could well have signalled the end of an illustrious career for Dean Richards.

a match for anyone and seem set to take honours before long – the Heineken Conference perhaps?

Leicester were the cup side of the season. Apart from their success in the Pilkington Cup, they helped to uphold the reputation of the English clubs by reaching the Heineken Cup final. After demolishing Toulouse in the last semi final at Welford Road, they were outplayed in the final at Cardiff Arms Park by Brive (28–9). With all their distractions it cannot be a surprise that the Tigers only finished fourth in the league.

The French domination of European club rugby was emphasised in the Heineken Conference in which they provided all four semi-finalists, but – bankrupcies permitting – English clubs have the capacity to reverse the trend.

Other clubs to show improvement at the top level over the season were Northampton and Saracens, while the RFU's fixture organisers must have breathed a sigh of relief that strugglers Bristol and London Irish won their relegation play-offs, since it seemed that this system was contrived during the season and might have led to legal arguments had there been different results.

Orrell and West Hartlepool were left well behind when the final tables of the season were completed and they are replaced by the well-bankrolled Richmond (unbeaten in the league) and Sir John Hall's Newcastle, whose progress will be watched with interest in the next campaign. There are intriguing newcomers to the renamed Premier League Two with Exeter accompanied by Fylde of Bill Beaumont fame.

Into the third division go two unbeaten League Four sides in Newbury from Four South and Worcester from Four North. Both are ambitious clubs and should do well – if not, their loyal supporters and backers will want to know why.

New entries from the junior ranks to senior status are Sedgley Park from the North, Hinckley (Midland Division), Esher (London in place of the luckless Charlton Park) and Bridgwater form the South West, who beat off the brave challenge of Cornwall's Launceston on points difference.

Matthew Singer touches down to consolidate Cambridge's lead in the Varsity match.

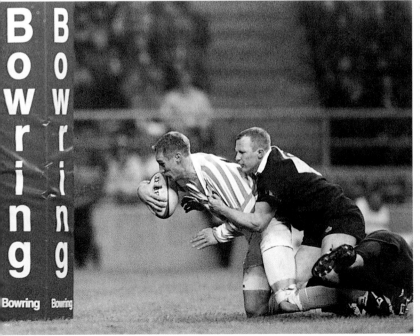

Elsewhere, the Varsity Match at Twickenham was again won by a good Cambridge side (23–7) with their excellent full back Matthew Singer going over for two superb tries. Oxford had lost an outstanding Australian prospect Ian Tucker, who died after a match at Saracens early in the season and an already difficult task was made even harder by the tragedy.

Loughborough again lost narrowly in the BUSA final to Brunel University College (9–8) and there was also a new name on the Hospitals Cup, which was won by a combination of Guy's and St Thomas', beating St Mary's by a comfortable 33–11 scoreline.

The Army narrowly won the Inter Services title, but the lads in red were extremely fortunate to win their Twickenham opener against the Royal

Brunel University College celebrate theior BUSA final victory over Loughborough.

Navy and later drew with the Royal Air Force, whose match against the Navy was also drawn. All three matches were narrow thrillers and the standard of services rugby, handicapped by defence cuts, was agreeably high.

It is also nice to report that the Barbarians still survive in spite of a total lack of cooperation from clubs in terms of releasing players for their matches. Unfortunately, they lost traditional opponents Cardiff and Swansea, but it is hoped that the new season will see this situation remedied.

The all-new Intermediate Cup final and the Junior Cup final (formerly known as the Pilkington Shield) produced two excellent Twickenham finals on the same day. Thanet Wanderers from Kent won the former with a 21–13 victory over Doncaster and Harpenden defeated Crewe & Natnwich 34–31 after extra-time in the latter.

The Middlesex 7s ended the competitive season in England and was won with embarrassing ease by a Fiji-dominated Barbarians seven, which may be against the spirit of the event since it was originally meant to be an end of season 'jolly' – and was there any harm in that? Indeed, attendances and the reputation of the competition had taken a slight hammering in recent seasons, but the temporary arrival of Wigan RLFC had done something to improve that and in future a proper club afternoon would be preferred by most.

I shall end this piece on a note of caution. There are still a number of internal disputes to be solved. Both Save & Prosper and Pilkington have departed the rugby scene as sponsors – were they pushed or did they volunteer? – and Courage will shortly follow. Their contribution to the game has been invaluable and one wonders whether it was always fully appreciated at headquarters. Will they be replaced by something better? Will relations with the non-terrestrial television companies be for the ultimate good of the game and how long will it take before England's fans have to pay even larger sums of money to watch the big games?

The RFU has a moral duty to keep fans happy and one hopes – possibly in vain – that the 'money' issue will not always be of more importance than the supporters' interests. It would be unwise, however, to expect too many favours.

performance
from

N E X T

WALES – Money leads the way

BY DAVID STEWART

In the first professional season Cardiff spent the most money and on paper had assembled the strongest squad. However, few would dispute the fact that the relative paupers of Pontypridd had the more satisfying record. Excluded from the latter stages of the Heineken Cup on points difference only, they put that disappointment behind them to win the Welsh National League by a clear margin from joint runners-up Swansea and Llanelli. Extremely difficult to beat at Sardis Road, well organised, with a high emphasis on loyalty to club and town they struck a blow for the less well resourced in the new moneyed era. Lions hero Neil Jenkins was, of course, their trump card leading the way both as captain and top scorer, extending his league points record in the process. His contribution was by no means the whole story. Continuity was an important factor. A settled squad blended the experience of recent international players Mark Rowley, Dale McIntosh and Paul John with shining new talents like full back Kevin Morgan (capped on the Welsh summer tour to North America) and wing Gareth Wyatt. Conducting the orchestra once again was coach Dennis John, father of Paul.

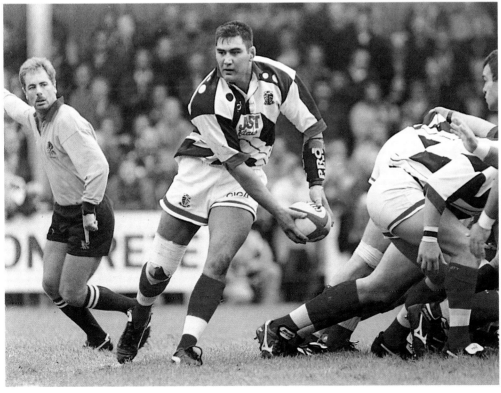

Neil Jenkins (above) finished as top points-scorer in the league, but it was a mix of recent internationals, such as Dale McIntosh (left) and talented youngsters that led Pontypridd to the title.

(Above) Director of rugby Terry Cobner was in favour of reducing the number of sides in the top flight from 12 to eight. .
(Below) Hemi Taylor lifts the SWALEC Cup.

The league season was somewhat controversial. Once again a bonus points system was in operation relative to the number of tries scored. It should be emphasised that under the traditional system of only two points for a win and one for a draw, Pontypridd would still have come out on top. Whether they can sustain their form in the new season remains to be seen – as others strengthen their squads it will not be easy. The other major contentious issue was the reduction of the first division from 12 to eight teams for the new season. This decision was taken at a Special General Meeting of the WRU halfway through last season. Director of rugby Terry Cobner considered the move essential to improve the competitiveness and quality of matches and raise playing standards. This late unexpected moving of the goalposts meant four teams would be relegated at the season's end, and none promoted. Financial arrangements were put in hand to compensate the unfortunate clubs affected, but the whole affair still left an air of bewilderment. Dunvant, Newbridge, Treorchy and Caerphilly will be playing second division rugby next year, along with Llandovery and Aberavon who would otherwise have been promoted.

Cardiff started the season with a number of new signings in David Young, Justin Thomas, Leigh Davies, Gwyn Jones and the jewel in their crown, the outstanding Robert Howley. Although only Howley played to a consistently high standard, Cardiff's investment did not go unrewarded. Their consolation was the SWALEC Cup. Sadly a wet day dampened the promise of a running game with Swansea on what was the final big match at the old National Stadium before the bulldozers moved in. A superb opportunist try by Olympic-athlete-turned-international-winger Nigel Walker was just enough to see Cardiff home despite a strong finish from the All Whites.

The Cup final aside, the two best remembered club games in Wales were the visits of Bath to Pontypridd and Cardiff respectively under the European banner. On each occasion full houses and a vibrant atmosphere saw the home sides triumph, proof were it needed that this competition has brought a new and welcomed dimension to northern hemisphere rugby. Cardiff's own Euro adventure ended in the January cold and snow of Brive at the semi-final stage. The French side subsequently came to the National Stadium and utterly outplayed Leicester in an exciting, well-attended final. Cardiff's response to the winners seems to have been 'if you can't beat 'em, buy 'em'. Their former second-row Tony Rees has returned to the club and brought with him the large and dynamic Polish exile Gregori Kacala whose pace, power and dexterity from the back row illuminated the final stages of last year's competition. Another returnee was Alex Evans now established as director of rugby in the new PLC set up. Terry Holmes will continue as coach.

Swansea won many friends for the style and adventure of their play throughout the season. Injury ravaged towards its close, many neutrals would have been happy to see them pull off another cup win. Theirs was another squad which demonstrated the benefits of continuity. Their players tried very hard to see off director of coaching Mike Ruddock with a trophy. Arguably the outstanding rugby thinker of recent years in Wales, Ruddock has a Dublin wife and headed across the Irish Sea to take up a contractual position with Leinster. Their prodigal was Lions centre Scott Gibbs returning to St Helens (by the beach) from St Helens (in the North) following the removal of rugby's Berlin Wall. Swansea, whilst facing the same financial worries as all their rivals, start the new season with John Plumtree as coach (recruited from Natal) and a talented squad headed by the experience of Gibbs, Tony Clement, Stuart Davies, Paul Arnold and supplemented by classy youngsters such as Chris Loader and Chris Anthony at prop and the North Walian Moore Brothers, Steve and Andy in the engine-room.

Llanelli faced greater monetary problems than most. Chairman Stewart Gallagher at one stage wrote to the membership indicating that the very survival of the club was in doubt. It was not easy for their players to operate against such a backdrop, but inspired by the effervescent and enterprising Gareth Jenkins once again as coach, well led by Rupert Moon, and controlled by Kiwi Frano Botica at fly half, they finished joint second in the league, just missed out to Cardiff in a classic cup semi-final, and progressed to the final stages of the European competition where alas the power of Brive (away) proved too much at the quarter-final stage. A good base of young players including the likes of Andrew Gibbs, Mike Voyle and two probable future internationals in Vernon Cooper (second row) and Hywel Jenkins (back row) bodes well.

Outside the top four clubs, the picture was rather bleaker, and looks like becoming increasingly so. Problems at the bank devilled Bridgend as well. It is conceivable that before long the Brewery Field club which once boasted the likes of JPR Williams and Steve Fenwick amongst a host of other internationals, may soon have no wearers of the red jersey within their ranks. At times they played exciting rugby, but struggled away from home undermining their challenge for a high league finish and Heineken Cup qualification. Neath, league winners a year earlier, struggled to avoid relegation. Barry Williams, having been selected for the Lions, demonstrated admirable loyalty in continuing to play for the club until safety was assured, notwithstanding his pending lucrative transfer to Richmond. As with Newport, they will be relying on a young and thus fairly inexpensive squad for the new season. The Black and Ambers, located in one of the fastest growing commercial towns in Europe, will hope to make progress under the off-field guidance of David Watkins and Tom David. Oddly enough Ebbw Vale may be best placed to challenge for a top four place next season. The highlight of their campaign was a cup semi-final appearance where they ran Swansea to the wire. With a settled squad led by Kingsley Jones and stable financing organised by the locally-born but London-based Russell brothers, their prospects look better than some.

Impressions of the season past? The predomination of European rugby over the domestic competitions; a clear banding of clubs in the first division between a top, middle, and lower foursome; improvements in the style and entertainment value of much of the rugby played; financial woes in abundance. The season ahead? An influx of second-tier southern hemisphere players to supplement the USA and Canadian internationals already within the ranks; the continuing battle between the leading clubs and the WRU; and crucially whether Welsh clubs will be competitive in Europe against French and especially the bigger multi-national English clubs.

SCOTLAND – Melrose set the standard

BY BILL McLAREN

Never in the proud 120 years history of Melrose Rugby Club, in the Scottish Border country, has there been such a season to remember as 1996–97, not even that inaugural event in 1883 when Melrose introduced to the world the seven-a-side game by staging the first-ever short game tournament at their beloved Greenyards.

Not since the days when Hawick dominated one National League campaign after another by winning the first five in a row and another five between 1982 and 1987 has one club so established itself as 'the one to beat' than Melrose in the past season when they achieved a unique treble by winning the SRU Tennents Premiership and Cup as well as the Border League championship. It was special icing on their cake that they also won their own 7s tournament, the 'Blue Riband' of the Scottish circuit. It provided further satisfaction at the Greenyards that Melrose set a new mark as Premiership champions with 14 wins in 14 games, Hawick (twice) and Gala once having achieved 100 per cent records, but not over 14 games.

When firing on all cylinders Melrose were arguably the one Scottish club side who might have made some impact in the European competition had the Scottish Rugby Union not opted for district representation there. Melrose were able to field five capped players in their back division in Rowen Shepherd, Derek Stark, Scott Nichol, Craig Chalmers and Bryan Redpath and also had capped forwards in Peter Wright, lock Stewart Campbell and Carl Hogg. Indeed every one of the first-choice Melrose XV had played for Scotland at one level or another and it underlined the quality of their reserve strength that, at times, they had on their bench Derek Bain, a midfield artiste who toured with Scotland in Australia in 1992, and back-five forward, Scott Aitken, who had played for Scotland 'A' in their 32–19 win over South Africa 'A' in November 1996. Melrose also benefited from having so many of their squad contracted to the SRU and thus being full-time players with daily squad sessions.

They could strike on all fronts with the style of total game that at times resembled the lively continuity of the Super 12 competition in the southern hemisphere. What the Melrose pack lacked in massive physical presence was compensated by overall forward mobility and cohesion, high skill levels and a dogged application towards their basic obligations as well as street wisdom in the ruder arts of forward play. Not only did they have Scotland's bench hooker Steve Brotherstone, but a loose-forward trio comprising a tough, mobile Australian, Michael Donnan, a capped No.8 in Carl Hogg and an uncompromising Kiwi rear gunner in Nick Broughton who toured with Scotland in his native country in 1996. There also was guidance from the worldly-wise lock Robbie Brown, veteran of some 235 first-team games and scorer of 52 tries – some haul for a denizen of the stoke room! Tactical direction was in the capable hands and feet of Chalmers and the captain Redpath who have played together in 15 cap internationals and who were giants at club level. They lit the touchpaper to some breathtaking interplay by very quick backs whose incisive operations were handsomely augmented by the vision and judgement of full back Rowen Shepherd whose confidence has heightened as his international experience has been extended. It was testimony to the flow of Melrose play that the top try-scorer in the upper divisions of the Premiership was their slim, nippy centre Nichol, with 16 whilst wing Stark notched 11. It demonstrated also how Melrose spread the load that, of their 82 Premiership tries, 24 were by their forwards. The interaction between their backs and forwards, with each taking on the other's role whenever required and with players taking the ball at pace, proved vital ingredients in the Melrose strategy when set alongside the willingness of every player to step on his accelerator in defence as much as in attack. There were occasions when Melrose touched heights of ball transference and weight of pass that most of their rivals found hard to match. There was, too, a prolific points-scorer in stocky cheekie chappie Gary Parker who amassed 171 before following in the footsteps of Gavin Hastings into American football. Parker always aimed to do the ball a painful injury with every kick, and was one of the club game's personalities.

Only Watsonians with 587 scored more Premiership points than Melrose who registered the most tries (82) and who were stretched only by the two clubs who seemed capable of toppling them, Watsonians and Boroughmuir.

Derreck Stark touches down to score the crucial try which gave Melrose victory over Watsonians.

Melrose had set a standard early on. They had drawn 26–26 with Newcastle who included Tony Underwood, Rob Andrew, Gary Armstrong, Nick Popplewell, Ross Nesdale, Doddie Weir, Gareth Archer, Peter Walton and Dean Ryan. They posted further warning in their first Premiership game by winning 107–10, 16 tries to one! The margin was startling enough, but what took the breath away more was that the opposition was Stirling County who had been champions and runners-up in the previous two seasons. Stirling had a series of crippling injuries to key men, including capped players Kevin McKenzie and Ian Jardine and missed the inspirational qualities of evergreen lock Stewart Hamilton. Nichol scored five of the Melrose tries and Parker kicked 13 goals. Stirling eventually ended up in bottom position in division one.

Melrose meanwhile saw off all their main challengers in the opening four weeks with

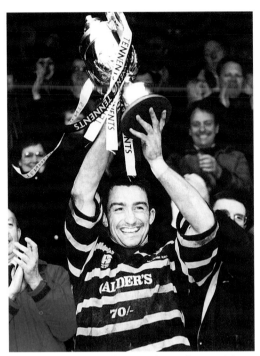

Bryan Redpath hoisrs the championship trophy clinched by Melrose after 14 straight wins.

defeats of Watsonians (27–26), Currie (35–19), Boroughmuir (47–25) and Hawick (35–13). Watsonians however, led Melrose by 10–0 and 20–10 before succumbing to that 27–26 margin at Merseyside. No side in Scotland typifies the adventurous spirit more than Watsonians who have moved the ball around in daring fashion since their captain of 1882–83 John Todd, proclaimed, 'I shall not have a man in the side who will not pass to his neighbour.' The modern-day Watsonians play with the same freedom of spirit and with the ideal personnel for that function: Derek Lee, successor to Gavin Hastings, quick and a livewire, now with London Scottish and in Scotland's tour party to South Africa in the summer; John Kerr, a far-ranging wing and lethal finisher; Scott Hastings, Scotland's most capped player with 64 and still a totally committed club man; Andrew Garry, a subtle play-maker and ideal foil to the Hastings bravado; Duncan Hodge, freely tipped as Scotland's next fly half and who was top points-scorer in the top divisions with 252; a 19-year-old centre of high potential in Jamie Mayer, who has the same solid build of his father Mike, a former Watsonians and Edinburgh prop – Jamie is a bit quicker! Watsonians, too, have achieved enviable mobility in their pack that includes the British Lions prop Tom Smith, a future Scottish lock in Stuart Grimes, an Aberdonian who has played five times for Scotland 'A', two New Zealand-born flankers in Cameron Mather (6ft 6ins) and Craig Brown (6ft 4ins) and a 20-year-old flanker, Iain Sinclair, nicknamed 'the fox terrier' who has captained Scotland at youth level and has been dubbed 'the Merseyside Neil Back'.

It stood to reason that the second Melrose versus Watsonians contest on 22 February would have an important influence upon the outcome of the Premiership. What a thriller it turned out to be with a crowd of 8,000 enthralled throughout as Watsonians came within a whisker of achieving a first win at the Greenyards since 1985 and of keeping the championship alive. It was a super advertisement for the top level of the Scottish club game. Watsonians were unlucky to lose through injury and 'flu respectively Scott Hastings and Mather, but Melrose did score four tries to one in a 26–22 victory, the vital score being sparked by a typical Chalmers mortar bomb to which Shepherd rose high like a salmon up a cauld before sending Parker clear.

So Melrose thus tied up the championship and all that remained was to clinch a 100 per cent record with victory over Currie at Malleny Park in the closing game. This they did by 37–22, Shepherd contributing a try, four conversions and two penalty goals. They were worthy champions with 28 title points to Watsonians' 24.

The one other club that hinted to threaten Melrose was Boroughmuir, but as often in the past they blew hot and cold, hot against the heavy artillery, cold against the lower order. All the same on 11 January, they created heart murmurs at Greenyards when they scored three tries to one and had the player of the game in their captain Stuart Reid, but six penalty goals by Parker eased Melrose out of jail by 23–19, Boroughmuir being penalised 21 times to Melrose's 12.

During their campaign, Boroughmuir had spells of wondrous interplay at pace with two old-head caps, Douglas Wyllie and Sean Lineen, as chief playmakers, Graeme Beveridge a 20-year-old beaver who asked questions at scrum half, Darren Burns, a

Scottish 'A' lock with springs in his heels, and a new personality in Alastair McLean, stocky and very sharp to the main chance, and a rare blend at breakaway in 20-year-old Alastair Cadzow, Reid, who was capped against Western Samoa in 1995, and Ron Kirkpatrick who played in the non-cap Test against Canada in 1991.

It was in the Cup that Boroughmuir came closest to true potential. They beat four division one sides on their way to the final – Hawick (19–6), Stirling County (71–9), Watsonians (42–29) and Heriots FP (45–0). That quarter-final defeat of Watsonians at Meggetland was an exceptional performance that involved a stunning display by the Boroughmuir full back Campbell Aitken, 6ft 3in, formerly of Heriot's FP. He scored three splendid tries, three conversions and two penalty goals for 27 points, the other tries being by McLean and Beveridge (2). Boroughmuir led at one stage by 35–10 which gave some credence to the words of their captain Reid that 'they were sick of being labelled under-achievers and of hearing about the two best clubs in Scotland being Melrose and Watsonians. We don't agree,' he said.

Yet it was Melrose who created history with the first league and cup double when, in the cup final, before a crowd of 23,000 at Murrayfield on 10 May, they beat Boroughmuir by 31–23 in a superbly entertaining match. It proved also a *tour de force* by Scotland's full back, Shepherd, who won the man of the match award with a 26-point haul from three tries, three penalty goals and one conversion. Boroughmuir were unfortunate to lose two key forward stalwarts, Kirkpatrick and Kevin Allan, formerly of Melrose, but they led 13–8 at the interval and had two cracking tries from the ever-improving McLean before Melrose's fitness and class told in the last quarter. It wasn't quite the farewell from active play that the likeable Sean Lineen would have chosen, but he had the satisfaction of setting up a try for his veteran colleague Wyllie and Lineen can look back on 29 caps and loyal service to club, district and country. He will be back at Murrayfield in the new season to help with the coaching.

The big question for 1997–98 is whether Melrose can continue to set the pace with all their rivals trailing in their wake. They have recruited well, but they are to lose their much respected coach Rob Moffat who toured as a wing with Scotland in the Far East in 1977 and who now moves on to coach the district side, the Border Reivers, for the district championship and the European Cup. His successor as coach is the 44-times capped Keith Robertson. Boroughmuir also lose their dedicated coach Henry Edwards who moves on to take charge of the Edinburgh district side.

In division two of the Premiership there was a dramatic finale as West of Scotland and Dundee High School FP locked horns on 29 March to decide who would gain promotion to division one. Dundee led 13–12 with time running out when international referee Ray Megson penalised Dundee for interference in the line out. Despite a bustling cross wind, veteran full back David Barrett piloted home his fifth penalty goal for a West victory by 15–13. So the West of Scotland club, 132 years old and spawning such kenspeckle capped men as Sandy Carmichael, the Brown brothers, Peter and Gordon, Alastair McHarg and Chris Rea, will accompany Edinburgh Academicals into division one and thus provide some promising young talents such as the Bulloch brothers, Alan and Gordon, the flying machine James Craig, Guy Perrett and David McLeish a taste of the top echelon as preparation for their further challenges at representative level.

There will be a change to the Premiership format in 1997–98 when the four divisions of eight clubs each will be replaced by three divisions of ten clubs. In any event there seems little doubt that it will take a monumental effort by their rivals to prevent Melrose and their talented squad from repeating their quite exceptional feats of season 1996–97.

IRELAND – Shannon continue monopoly

BY SEAN DIFFLEY

For the first time in the eight-year history of the event there will be a play-off for the All Ireland League title this season. The top club in the 14-team first division will play off against the fourth-placed club and the second-placed will have a semi-final joust with the third-placed. The first- and second-placed sides will have home advantage and the final will take place at Lansdowne Road.

There will also be substantial financial rewards for those reaching the play-offs and a new sponsor. Allied Irish Banks, who have replaced the Insurance Corporation of Ireland as sponsors, are said to have increased the total finance now available to a competition that lost its intensity last season. There were all sorts of suggestions from many sources advocating a change in the format of the league. There were those who felt an eight-team first division would be the best solution. However, a sub-committee comprising representatives from the clubs in all four divisions, under the chairmanship of IRFU vice president Noel Murphy, decided on retaining the format, but recommended that at the end of the season three teams will be automatically relegated and in the 1998–99 season the first division will be reduced to 12 clubs.

Leinster's Martin Ridge takes on Mick Lynch of Munster (12) during the match at Donnybrook, Dublin.

That the new format and the announcement of the new sponsors only came towards the end of July spoke volumes about the amount of debate among the clubs and the difficulties the IRFU had in marrying up the various suggestions and demands. The fundamental difficulty, of course, was that the standards in the All Ireland were not comparable at all to the highly successful competition of the previous eight years. And the simple reason for that was that nearly all of Ireland's leading players were playing their club rugby in England

So, club standards suffered, though in fairness the problems were also influenced by a rash decision to break the league fixture list with a long interval in mid-season. By the time action recommenced, the rugby public had forgotten what had occurred earlier and enthusiasm among the supporters was fairly lax, certainly in comparison with previous seasons, and interest in the league took a nosedive.

Another move by the IRFU to keep its leading players at

home was the offer of contracts to the four provinces. Ulster, Leinster and Munster are, as before, involved in the European Cup and Connacht are in the European Conference. Each of the four is being subsidised by the IRFU to contract 30 players and the IRFU has undertaken to pay full-time players £25,000 plus various bonuses and to pay those remaining part-time players £7,500 plus fees. In the first list issued also in late July there were 76 players named, with 15 of those announced as full time. The only notables on that list were Mick Galwey, Anthony Foley and Mark McCall.

The IRFU president, the former Lion and Ireland wing Niall Brophy, said that the move was a 'critical step in the Union's programme to re-establish Ireland as a major force on the field of world rugby'.

And while all that was going on, the cross-channel based players, through their agents, were discussing contracts with the Union in Dublin. All that was concerned with the original offers made in May or packages worth something over £70,000 which, the grapevine had it, did not impress the players – or their agents – very much.

Meanwhile, on the Irish club front, the big question again was – could any side end the All Ireland monopoly of the Limerick clubs? Shannon won the competition last season for the third consecutive year, winning 12 of their 13 matches with a commitment, enthusiasm and pride that left all the rest foundering in their wake.

Three Leinster clubs, Lansdowne, coached by Donal Spring, Terenure College, by the former Irish coach Gerry Murphy, and St Mary's College with Ciaran Fitzgerald at the coaching helm for his last season, were locked together six points behind Shannon, with Ballymena a further point in arrears. The successful Shannon coach was their former No.8 Niall O'Donovan who will now take over the post as the Munster provincial coach.

Mick Galwey (above) was one of the few notable names to appear on the IRFU's list of full-time players.

The two relegated from division one were Old Wesley and Instonians who were replaced in the top division by Clontarf, the Dublin side and Dolphin from Cork. NIFC and Highfield went down from division two and up came the two Connacht sides, Buccaneers and Galwegians. The strength of the various junior provincial leagues was demonstrated by Suttonians from Leinster and Ballynahinch from Ulster gaining promotion to division three after only gaining a place in the All Ireland the previous season. For next season the provincial sides promoted were Carlow from Leinster and Omagh from Ulster. They take over the places in division four vacated by Armagh and University College Galway.

FRANCE – Four in a row for Toulouse

BY CHRIS THAU

For a glorious weekend at the end of the spring, Paris, invaded by the colourful cohorts of supporters, becomes the biggest provincial city of France. For the fourth time in a row, the Toulouse hordes commandeered the bistros and cafes of St Lazare, St Claude and Auteuil, while the more cautious visitors from Bourgoin, on their first-ever trip to Parc des Princes, confined themselves to the small hotels on the outskirts of the city.

The match was a grim affair, in which Toulouse's defensive pragmatism prevailed over Bourgoin's flamboyant, yet inexperienced romanticism – admittedly without Stephane Glas, who was injured after 22 minutes. It was the fourth final in the history of the centenary competition (this was the 96th championship final) without a try. After a

Silvain Dispagne in action for Toulouse against Leicester in the Heineken Cup semi-final. European disappointmenr, however, was compensated by their fourth consecutive Bouclier de Brennus.

spectacular Grand Slam, a symbol of French creativity and *joie de vivre*, the championship final was a genuine anti-climax. Although captain courageous Marc Cecillon, in his last appearance for the club he reinvented, battled like a young lion, the Bourgoin forwards failed to break the stranglehold of the Toulouse pack, led by Sylvian Dispagne. Elsewhere their efforts were doomed. Toulouse, orchestrated by their master conductor and skipper Christophe Deylaud, simply locked them out.

Mind you the lack of style did not dampen the enthusiasm of the Toulouse supporters, and of the Toulouse players for that matter. As former national coach Pierre Berbizier had observed before the match in his *L'Equipe* column, 'In the final, the most important thing is to win.' The supporters donning red and black scarves, hats, shirts and trousers drank the city dry, while the players partied till the small hours of the following morning. It was Toulouse's 14th championship title, and fourth consecutive Bouclier de Brennus.

To reach the final, the first in its history, Bourgoin, the winner of the European Conference, beat Béziers 23–14 in the eighths, Pau 24–18 in the quarter-finals and Montferrand, last year's finalists, 21–17 in the semis. Toulouse survived a spirited challenge from Narbonne to win 24–22 in the eighths, beat neighbours Colomiers 21–12 in the quarters and overcome Agen in controversial circumstances 23–16 in the semi-final. In the final, Toulouse captain Christophe Deylaud landed three penalties and a dropped goal, to Geany's two penalties.

Unfortunately, the final was memorable for other reasons than its rugby. This was the last French championship final to be played at the Parc des Princes. Next year's final will be played at the new 80,000 seater Stade de France. It was also the last final of a mammoth 64-club French first division. As from the next season the French first division will have 20 clubs, divided into two pools of ten. In pool one, Toulouse, and the Heineken Cup champions Brive, Montferrand, Dax, Colomiers, Narbonne, Biarritz, Béziers, Nice and surprisingly La Rochelle, among the élite for the first time after about 30 years of peripheral existence in group A2. In pool two, Bourgoin are joined by Agen, Pau, Bègles, Perpignan, Castres, Toulon, Grenoble, Stade Français and Montpellier.

The new championship format is the first step by the FFR to attempt to structure the season, and to include the European Cups. Next year, the top 20 clubs will play 18 fixtures each (home and away) in their pools, followed by a number of knock-out matches, to determine both the champion at the top end, and the four relegated clubs at the bottom. In order to streamline the competition further, the first division will have 16 clubs next season, with a view of reducing it to 12 clubs after the 1999 Rugby World Cup.

Next season, there will be 20 clubs in the first division, and 20 in the second, conveniently called A2. In the third division there will be 48 clubs, divided into four pools of 12, while in the fourth division there are 112 clubs (eight pools of 14). In the fifth division there are 178 clubs playing in 16 pools (14 of 12 clubs each and 2 of 11 clubs). Below the fifth division, there are several regional competitions involving the remainder of approximately 1,500 French clubs. This rather strong pyramid, with a very wide base, may help to explain the steady stream of talent reaching the top of the French game, and ultimately the consistent success of France at international level

French domination in Europe was confirmed by Brive's success in the Heineken Cup and by France claiming the Grand Slam in the Five Nations.

There's no Taste like Heinz

FIXTURES 1997–98

AUGUST 1997

Sat, 16th — Welsh Nat Lgs Premier & 1st Divs
Irish Inter Prov. Championship
  Connacht v Munster (Galway)
  Leinster v Ulster (Dublin)

Sat, 23rd — English Premier League 1
Welsh Nat Lgs Premier & 1st Divs
Irish Inter Prov. Championship
  Connacht v Ulster (Galway)
  Munster v Leinster (TBA)

Wed, 27th — Wales 'A' v Romania

Sat, 30th — WALES v ROMANIA (Wrexham)
English Premier League 1
English Premier League 2
Scottish 'League Trophy' Gps A & B
Irish Inter Prov. Championship
  Leinster v Connacht (Dublin)
  Ulster v Munster (Belfast)

SEPTEMBER 1996

Sat, 6th — Heineken Cup & Conference
English Premier League
Scottish 'League Trophy' Gps A & B
Welsh Swalec Cup Prelim. Round
Welsh Nat League Div 1
Welsh Nat League Divs 2,3,4

Sat, 13th — Heineken Cup & Conference
English Knock-Out Cups - S,I,J
English Premier League
Scottish 'League Trophy' Gps A & B
SRU Tennents Cup Round Three
Welsh Nat League Div 1
Welsh Nat League Divs 2,3,4

Sat, 20th — Heineken Cup & Conference
English Premier League 2
English National League 1
English National League 2
Scottish 'League Trophy' Gps A & B (4) Scotland
SRU Tennents National Lgs Divs 1-7
Welsh Nat League Div 1
Welsh Nat League Divs 2,3,4

Sat, 27th — Heineken Cup & Conference
English Premier League 2
Scottish 'League Trophy' Gps A & B
Tennents National Lgs Divs 1-7
Welsh Swalec Cup First Round

Welsh Nat League Div 1
Welsh Nat League Divs 2,3,4

OCTOBER 1996

Sat, 4th — English Knock-Out Cups - S,I,J
Heineken Cup & Conference
English Premier League 2
Scottish 'League Trophy' Gps A & B
SRU Tennents National Lgs Divs 1-7
Welsh Nat League Div 1
Welsh Nat League Divs 2,3,4

Sat, 11th — Heineken Cup & Conference
English Premier League 2
Scottish 'League Trophy' Gps A & B
SRU Tennents Cup Round Three
Welsh Nat League Div 1
Welsh Nat League Divs 2,3,4

Sat, 18th — English Premier League 1
English Premier League 2
English National League 1
English National League 2
Scottish 'League Trophy' Gps A & B
SRU Tennents National Lgs Divs 1-7
Welsh Swalec Cup Second Round
Welsh Nat League Div 1
Welsh Nat League Divs 2,3

Sat, 25th — English Premier League 1
English Premier League 2
Scottish 'League Trophy' Gps A & B
SRU Tennents National Lgs Divs 1-7
Welsh Nat League Premier Div
Welsh Nat League Div 1
Welsh Nat League Divs 2,3
Welsh Nat League Div 4 (7)

NOVEMBER 1997

Sat, 1st — Heineken Cup & Conference (QF)
English Knock-Out Cups - S,I,J
SRU Tennents National Lgs Divs 1-7
Welsh Nat League Premier Div
Welsh Nat League Div 1
Welsh Nat League Div 2,3
Welsh Nat League Div 4 (8)

Sat, 8th — Heineken Cup & Conference (QF)
Llanelli v New Zealand (Llanelli)
English Premier League 1

English Premier League 2
Welsh Nat League Div 1
Welsh Nat League Divs 2,3
Welsh Nat League Div 4

Sun, 9th SRU Tennents Cup Round Three
SRU Tennents Bowl Prelim.
Round

Tues, 11th Wales 'A' v New Zealand
(Cardiff)

Sat, 15th ENGLAND v AUSTRALIA
IRELAND v NEW ZEALAND
English Premier Leagues 1 & 2
L/Cup
English National League 1
English National League 2
SRU Tennents Premiership Divs
1,2,3
SRU Tennents National Lgs Divs
1-7

Tue, 18th Emerging England v New
Zealand (TBA)

Sat, 22nd ENGLAND v NEW ZEALAND
Old Trafford (Manchester)
SCOTLAND v AUSTRALIA
English Knock-Out Cups - I,J
English Premier Leagues 1 & 2
L/Cup
English National League 1
English National League 2
SRU Tennents National Lgs Divs
1-7
Welsh Swalec Cup Third Round
Welsh Nat League Div 1
AIL Championship

Mon, 24th Dubai Sevens (two days)

Tue, 25th WALES v TONGA (Llanelli)
Allied Dunbar XV v
New Zealand (Bristol)

Sat, 29th ENGLAND v SOUTH AFRICA
WALES v NEW ZEALAND
(Wembley)
English Premier Leagues 1 & 2
L/Cup
English County Championships
SRU Tennents Premiership Divs
1,2,3
SRU Tennents National Lgs Divs
1-7
Welsh Nat League Div 1
Welsh Nat League Divs 2,3
Welsh Nat League Div 4

DECEMBER 1997

Tue, 2nd England 'A' v New Zealand
(Leicester)

Sat, 6th ENGLAND v NEW ZEALAND
SCOTLAND v SOUTH AFRICA
IRELAND v CANADA
English Premier Leagues 1 & 2

L/Cup
English County Championships
Welsh Nat League Divs 2,3
Welsh Nat League Div 4
AIL Championship

Sun, 7th SRU Tennents Cup Round Four
SRU Tennents Shield & Bowl R1

Tue, 9th Oxford v Cambridge
(Twickenham)
Oxford v Cambridge (U21s)
(Stoop Memorial Ground)

Sat, 13th English Premier League 1
English Premier League 2
English County Championships
SRU Tennents Premiership Divs
1,2,3
SRU Tennents National Lgs Divs
1-7
Welsh Nat League Premier Div
Welsh Nat League Div 1
Welsh Nat League Divs 2,3
Welsh Nat League Div 4
AIL Championship

Sat, 20th ITALY v IRELAND
Heineken Cup & Conference (SF)
English Premier League 1
English Premier League 2
English National League 1
English National League 2
SRU Tennents Premiership Divs
1,2,3
Welsh Nat League Premier Div
Welsh Nat League Div 1
Welsh Swalec Cup Fourth Round

Sat, 27th English Premier League 1
English National League 1
English National League 2
SRU Tennents Premiership Divs
1,2,3
Welsh Nat League Premier Div
Welsh Nat League Div 1
Welsh Nat League Divs 2,3
Welsh Nat League Div 4
AIL Championship Ireland

Tue, 30th English Premier League 1

JANUARY 1998

Sat, 3rd English Knock-Out Cup - Senior
English Knock-Out Cup - I,J
English National League 1
English National League 2
Welsh Nat League Premier Div
Welsh Nat League Div 1
Welsh Nat League Divs 2,3
Welsh Nat League Div 4
AIL Championship

Sat, 10th English Premier League 1
English Premier League 2
English National League 1

	English National League 2
	SRU Tennents Premiership Divs 1,2,3
	SRU Tennents National Lgs Divs 1-7
	Welsh Nat League Div 1
	Welsh Nat League Divs 2,3
	Welsh Nat League Div 4
	AIL Championship
Sun,11th	Uruguay Sevens (two days)
Sat, 17th	English Premier League 1
	English Premier League 2
	English National League 1
	English National League 2
	SRU Tennents Premiership Divs 1,2,3
	SRU Tennents National Lgs Divs 1-7
	Welsh Nat League Div 1
	Welsh Nat League Divs 2,3
	Welsh Nat League Div 4
	AIL Championship
Sat, 24th	English Knock-Out Cup - Senior
	English Knock-Out Cup - I,J
	English National League 1
	English National League 2
	Welsh Swalec Cup Fifth Round
	AIL Championship
Sun, 25th	SRU Tennents National Lgs Divs 1-7
Sat, 31st	Heineken Cup & Conference (F)
	English Premier League 1
	English Premier League 2
	English National League 1
	English National League 2
	SRU Tennents National Lgs Divs 1-7
	Welsh Nat League Premier Div
	Welsh Nat League Div 1
	Welsh Nat League Div 4
	AIL Championship

FEBRUARY 1998

Fri, 6th	Ireland 'A' v Scotland 'A'
	Ireland U21 v Scotland U21
	France 'A' v England 'A'
	England Stud v France Stud
Sat, 7th	FRANCE v ENGLAND
	IRELAND v SCOTLAND
	WALES v ITALY (TBA)
	English Premier League 1 & 2 L/Cup
	English National League 1
	English National League 2
Sat, 14th	English Premier League 1
	English Premier League 2
	English National League 1
	English National League 2
	SRU Tennents Premiership Divs

	1,2,3
	SRU Tennents National Lgs Divs 1-7
	Welsh Nat League Premier Div
	Welsh Nat League Div 1
	Welsh Nat League Divs 2,3,4
	AIL Championship
Fri, 20th	Scotland 'A' v France 'A'
	Scotland U21 v France U21
	England Stud v Wales Stud
Sat, 21st	ENGLAND v WALES
	SCOTLAND v FRANCE
	English Premier League 1 & 2 L/Cup
	English National League 1
	English National League 2
	AIL Championship
Sat, 28th	English Knock-Out Cup - S, I, J (QF)
	English County Championships (QF)
	SRU Tennents National Lgs Divs 1-7
	SRU Tennents Cup Round Five
	SRU Tennents Shield & Bowl R2
	Welsh Swalec Cup R6
	AIL Championship

MARCH 1997

Fri, 6th	Wales 'A' v Scotland 'A'
	Wales U21 v Scotland U21
	France 'A' v Ireland 'A'
	France U21 v Ireland U21
Sat, 7th	FRANCE v IRELAND
	WALES v SCOTLAND (Wembley)
	English Premier League 1
	English Premier League 2
	English National League 1
	English National League 2
	Wales Youth v England Colts
Sat, 14th	English Premier League 1
	English Premier League 2
	English National League 1
	English National League 2
	SRU Tennents National Lgs Divs 1-7
	Welsh Nat League Div 1
	Welsh Nat League Divs 2,3,4
	AIL Championship
Fri, 20th	Ireland 'A' v Wales 'A'
	Ireland U21 v Wales U21
	Scotland 'A' v England 'A'
	Scotland U21 v England U21
Sat, 21st	IRELAND v WALES
	English Premier League 1 & 2 L/C
	English National League 1
	English National League 2
Sun, 22nd	SCOTLAND v ENGLAND
	England Colts v Scotland U18

Wed, 25th	BUSA Finals - Men and Women Twickenham
Fri, 27th	Hong Kong Sevens (3 days)
Sat, 28th	English Knock-Out Cups - S,I,J - (SF)
	English County Championships - (SF)
	SRU Tennents National Lgs Divs 1-7
	Welsh Nat League Div 1
	Welsh Nat League Divs 2,3,4
	AIL Championship

APRIL 1997

Thu, 2nd	England 'A' v Wales 'A'
Fri, 3rd	England 'A' v Ireland 'A'
	England U21 v Ireland U21
	Wales 'A' v France 'A'
	Wales U21 v France U21
	England v Wales (18 Group)
Sat, 4th	ENGLAND v IRELAND
	English Premier League 1 & 2 L/Cup
	English National Leagues 2
	English Divisional League 12s
	SRU Tennents Cup, Shield & Bowl (QF)
Sun, 5th	WALES v FRANCE (Wembley)
Sat, 11th	English Premier League 1
	English Premier League 2
	English National League 1 & 2
	Welsh Swalec Cup (QF)
	Welsh Nat League Div 1
	AIL Championship
Sat, 18th	English County Champ. Final
	English Premier League 1
	English Premier League 2
	Welsh Nat League Premier Div
	Welsh Nat League Div 1
	Welsh Nat League Divs 2,3,4
	England v Ireland (18 Group)
Sun, 19th	SRU Tennents Cup, Shield & Bowl S/Fnls
Sat, 25th	Royal Navy v The Army
	English Premier League 1
	English Premier League 2
	English National League 1
	English National League 2
	Welsh Swalec Cup (SF)
	Welsh Nat League Div 1
	Welsh Nat League Divs 2,3,4
	England Colts v France Youth

MAY 1997

Sat, 2nd	English Knock-Out Cups - I,J Finals
	English Premier League 1
	Welsh Nat League Premier Div
	Welsh Nat League Div 1

Wed, 6th	Royal Navy v RAF (Twickenham)
Sat, 9th	English Senior Knock-Out Final
	RU Tennents Cup, Shield & Bowl Finals
	Welsh Nat Leaue Premier Div
	Welsh Nat League Div 1
Sun, 10th	English Premier League 1
Wed, 13th	The Army v RAF (Twickenham)
Sat, 16th	Middlesex Sevens finals
	English Premier League 1
	Welsh Nat League Premier Div
	Welsh Nat League Div 1
Sat, 23rd	Welsh SWALEC Cup final (Wembley)

A SUMMARY OF THE SEASON

BY BILL MITCHELL

INTERNATIONAL RUGBY

AUSTRALIA IN ITALY AND BRITISH ISLES (OCT–DEC 1996)

Opponents		Results
Italy 'A'	W	55-19
ITALY	W	40-18
Scotland 'A'	W	47-20
Glasgow-Edinburgh	W	37-19
Scottish Select XV	W	25- 9
SCOTLAND	W	29-19
Connacht	W	37-20
Ulster	W	39-26
Leinster	cancelled	
IRELAND	W	22-12
Munster	W	55-19
WALES	W	28-19
Barbarians	W	39-12

Played 12 Won 12 (one cancelled)

WESTERN SAMOA IN ENGLAND, IRELAND & WALES NOVEMBER & DECEMBER 1996

Opponents		Results
Saracens	L	40–53
Oxford University	W	58-27
Munster	W	35-25
IRELAND	W	40-25
Cambridge Univ.	W	13-12
Llanelli	L	15-23
Cardiff	W	53-29
Newbury	W	35-21
Bath	L	17-36
Leicester & N'ton	W	33-20
Richmond	W	32-12

Played 11 Won 8 Lost 3

ARGENTINA IN ENGLAND NOVEMBER & DECEMBER 1996

Opponents		Results
London Division	W	63-20
Western Counties	W	25-17
Midland Counties	W	90-24
Northern Counties	W	64-16
Combined Services	W	52- 6
England 'A'	L	17-22
ENGLAND	W	20-18

Played 7 Won 5 Lost 2

SOUTH AFRICA 'A' IN BRITISH ISLES NOVEMBER & DECEMBER 1996

Opponents		Results
Cambridge Univ.	W	57-11
Scotland 'A'	L	19-32
Ireland 'A'	L	25-28
Oxford University	W	49-12
London Counties	W	43-17
Northern Counties	W	29-13
Midland Counties	W	62 -7
Cardiff	W	40- 7
England 'A'	W	35-20
Emerging Wales	W	42-26

Played 11 Won 9 Lost 2

QUEENSLAND IN ENGLAND, SCOTLAND & WALES NOVEMBER & DECEMBER 1996

Opponents		Results
Cambridge Univ.	L	20-27
Michael Lynagh XV	W	27-18
Midland Counties	W	29-25
SW Counties	W	30- 9
London Counties	W	64-16
Pontypridd	W	28-19
Scottish Devel. XV	W	63-21
England 'A'	W	25-22

Played 8 Won 7 Lost 1

NEW ZEALAND BARBARIANS IN ENGLAND NOVEMBER 1996

Opponents		Results
Northern Counties	W	80- 0
ENGLAND	W	34-19

Played 2 Won 2

SOUTH AFRICA IN ARGENTINA, FRANCE & WALES OCTOBER TO DECEMBER 1996

Opponents		Results
Rosario	W	45-36
ARGENTINA	W	46-15
Cuyo	W	89-19
ARGENTINA	W	44-21

French Barbarians	L	22-30
South East France	W	36-20
FRANCE	W	22-12
French Universities	L	13-20
FRANCE (2nd Test)	W	13-12
WALES	W	37-20

Played 10 Won 8 Lost 2

UNITED STATES IN WALES
JANUARY 1997

Opponents	Results	
Emerging Wales	cancelled	
Neath	L	15-39
Pontypridd	W	15-13
WALES	L	14-34

Played 3 Won 1 Lost 2

OTAGO IN ENGLAND & SCOTLAND
JANUARY & FEBRUARY 1997

Opponents	Results	
Cambridge Univ.	W	47-23
London Irish	W	82-14
Scottish Devel. XV	W	44-19
England 'A'	W	42-15
Bath	W	31-18
Leicester & N'ton	W	37- 8
Richmond	W	70- 0

Played 7 Won 7

AUCKLAND BLUES IN ENGLAND & FRANCE

Opponents	Results	
Bristol	W	62-21
Harlequins	W	33-29
Brive	W	47-11

Played 3 Won 3

BRITISH ISLES IN SOUTH AFRICA
MAY TO JULY 1997

Opponents	Results	
Eastern Province	W	39-11
Border	W	18-14
Western Province	W	38-21
Mpumalanga	W	64-14
Northern Transvaal	L	30-35
Gauteng Lions	W	20-14
Natal Sharks	W	42-12
Emerging 'Boks	W	51-22
SOUTH AFRICA	W	25-16
Free State	W	50-32
SOUTH AFRICA	W	18-15
Northern Free State	W	76-39
SOUTH AFRICA	L	16-35

Played 13 Won 11 Lost 2

ENGLAND IN ARGENTINA
MAY & JUNE 1997

Opponents	Results	
Cordoba	W	38-21
Buenos Aires XV	L	21-23
Argentina 'A'	W	58-17
ARGENTINA	W	46-20
Cuyo	W	37- 8
ARGENTINA	L	13-33

Played 6 Won 4 Lost 2

WALES IN NORTH AMERICA
JULY 1997

Opponents	Results	
Sours	W	94 -3
UNITED STATES	W	30-20
US Development XV	W	56-23
UNITED STATES	W	28-23
Ontario	W	54-10
CANADA	W	28-25

Played 6 Won 6 Lost 0

ENGLAND U21 IN AUSTRALIA
JUNE/JULY 1997

Opponents	Results	
ACT	W	45-17
Queensland	L	21-43
New South Wales	L	12-31
Victoria	W	69-32
AUSTRALIA	L	7-27

Played 5 Won 2 Lost 3

SCOTTISH SILVER THISTLES IN
NEW ZEALAND JUNE/JULY 1997

Opponents	Results	
Thames Valley	D	29-29
Waikato U21	W	41-21
Counties 'B'	W	47-32
Harlequins XV	W	52-36

Played 4 Won 3 Drawn 1

ENGLAND SCHOOLS (18 Group) in
AUSTRALIA JULY – AUGUST 1997

Opponents	Results	
Northern Territories U20	W	115 -3
New South Wales Country	W	72 -8
ACT	W	41 -3
New South Wales HS	W	65 -5
Victoria	W	111 -0
Queensland	W	54 -8
Queensland Select	W	48 -15
AUSTRALIA	W	38-20

Played 7 Won 7 Lost 0

THE FIVE NATIONS CHAMPIONSHIP 1997

Results

Ireland	15	France	32
Scotland	19	Wales	34
England	41	Scotland	13
Wales	25	Ireland	26
France	27	Wales	22
Ireland	6	England	46
England	20	France	23
Scotland	38	Ireland	10
France	47	Scotland	20
Wales	13	England	34

	P	W	L	F	A	Trs	Pts
France	4	4	0	129	77	13	8
England	4	3	1	141	55	14	6
Wales	4	1	3	94	106	11	2
Scotland	4	1	3	90	132	9	2
Ireland	4	1	3	57	141	4	2

OTHER INTERNATIONAL MATCHES 1996-97

FULL INTERNATIONAL RESULTS

Australia	25	England	6

PAN AMERICAN TOURNAMENT

Argentina	29	U.S.A.	26
Canada	24	Uruguay	18
Argentina	54	Uruguay	20
Canada	23	U.S.A.	18
Canada	21	Argentina	41
U.S.A.	27	Uruguay	13

	P	W	L	F	A	Pts
Argentina	3	3	0	124	67	12
Canada	3	2	1	68	77	8
U.S.A.	3	1	2	71	65	4
Uruguay	3	0	3	51	105	1

Wales	33	France	40
England	54	Italy	21
Hong Kong	11	Fiji	64
Hong Kong	16	Fiji	37
Italy	22	Wales	31
Scotland	29	Italy	22
Ireland	29	Italy	37
France	32	Italy	40

(FIRA Championships)

Zimbabwe	12	Tonga	42
Romania	20	France	51

(FIRA CHAMPIONSHIPS)

South Africa	74	Tonga	10
New Zealand	71	Fiji	5
Zimbabwe	52	Italy	39
W. Samoa	62	Tonga	13
W. Samoa	26	Fiji	17

PACIFIC RIM CHAMPIONSHIP

Hong Kong	42	Japan	20
Canada	53	USA	14
Hong Kong	49	USA	9
Japan	32	Canada	31
Hong Kong	27	Canada	35
Japan	12	USA	20
USA	51	Japan	29
Canada	17	Hong Kong	16
Canada	42	Japan	18
USA	17	Hong Kong	14
USA	11	Canada	22
Japan	23	Hong Kong	41

	P	W	L	F	A	Pts
Canada	6	5	1	200	118	21
Hong Kong	6	3	3	189	121	14
USA	6	3	3	122	179	12
Japan	6	1	5	134	227	4

BLEDISLOE CUP

New Zealand	30	Australia	13

'A' INTERNATIONAL RESULTS

Scotland	56	Wales	11
Ireland	23	France	44
England	52	Scotland	17
Wales	34	Ireland	14
France	41	Wales	6
Ireland	30	England	44
England	25	France	34
Scotland	33	Ireland	34
France	23	Scotland	9
Romania	33	Wales	42

UNDER 21 INTERNATIONAL RESULTS

Scotland	41	Italy	15
Scotland	13	Wales	24
Ireland	13	France	40
England	35	Scotland	26
Wales	44	Ireland	14
France	51	Wales	20
Ireland	28	England	27
England	13	France	20
Scotland	0	Ireland	31
France	46	Scotland	6

STUDENT AND UNIVERSITY MATCHES 1996-97

Scotland Univ.	16	Wales Univ.	67
England Univ.	39	Scotland Univ.	13
Wales Univ.	11	Ireland Univ.	19
Scotland Univ.	5	Ireland Univ.	27
England Studs	14	France Studs	25
Wales Univ.	28	England Univ.	17

SCHOOLS 18 GROUP MATCHES 1996-97

France	42	Scotland	8
Scotland	15	Wales	17
England	20	France	10
Ireland	9	England	16
France	23	Wales	15
Wales	25	Ireland	27
England	55	Scotland	18
Wales	17	England	18
Scotland	11	Ireland	48

ALWAYS ONE TO SPOT A GOOD OPENING, ONCE ARCHIE HEARD ABOUT SAVE & PROSPER UNIT TRUSTS, THERE WAS NO STOPPING HIM

If you'd like to hear more about Save & Prosper Unit Trusts, just ring us on our free Moneyline: 0800 829 100. It could be just the break you need.

SAVE & PROSPER

WORLD YOUTH CHAMPIONSHIP

Semi-finals

Argentina	42	Ireland	0
France	40	Wales	12

Third place play-off

Wales	30	Ireland	17

Final

Argentina	18	France	12

CATHAY PACIFIC-HONGKONG BANK SEVENS

Melrose Cup Final

Fiji	24	South Africa 21	

Plate Final

Tonga	40	Hong Kong	19

Bowl Final

USA	40	Japan	28

Other major Sevens finals:

Paris:

Fiji	38	France	19

Japan:

Fiji	54	NZ Selection 19	

WOMENS MATCHES 1996–1997

Results

Scotland	10	Wales	0
England	23	Scotland	3
Wales	32	Ireland	5
Ireland	0	England	37
Scotland	28	Ireland	3
Wales	14	England	22

	P	W	L	F	A	Pts
England	3	3	0	82	17	6
Scotland	3	2	1	41	26	4
Wales	3	1	2	46	37	2
Ireland	3	0	3	8	97	0

Other international

France	6	England	15

European Championship

Semi-finals

France	10	England	15
Scotland	11	Spain	10

Final

England	24	Scotland	8

Other Internationals

England	17	Spain	15
Scotland 'A'	27	Wales 'A'	7
England 'A'	19	Scotland 'A'	8
England	15	France	17

TRI-NATIONS TOURNAMENT

South Africa	32	New Zealand	35
Australia	18	New Zealand	33
Australia	32	South Africa	20
New Zealand	55	South Africa	35
New Zealand	36	Australia	24
South Africa	61	Australia	22

	P	W	D	L	F	A	Pts
New Zealand	4	4	0	1	159	109	18
South Africa	4	1	0	3	148	144	7
Australia	4	1	0	3	96	150	6

CLUB, COUNTY AND DIVISIONAL RUGBY

ENGLAND

Pilkington Cup

Quarter-finals

Harlequins	28	Saracens	21
Newcastle	8	Leicester	18
Northampton	9	Sale	22
Wakefield	21	Gloucester	25

Semi-finals

Gloucester	13	Leicester	26
Sale	26	Harlequins	16

Final

Leicester	9	Sale	3

Junior Cup Final

Harpenden	34	Crewe & Nant.	31

(after extra time)

Intermediate Cup Final

Thanet Wanderers	21	Doncaster	13

Courage Leagues

Division 1

	P	W	D	L	F	A	Pts
Wasps	22	18	1	3	685	406	37
Bath	22	15	1	6	863	411	31
H'quins	22	15	0	7	745	416	30
Leicester	22	14	1	7	600	395	29
Sale	22	13	2	7	603	525	28
Saracens	22	12	1	9	568	449	25
Gloucester	22	11	1	10	476	589	23
N'ton	22	10	0	12	515	477	20
Bristol	22	8	1	13	432	625	17
London I.	22	6	0	16	502	747	12
W. H'pool	22	3	0	19	382	795	6
Orrell	22	3	0	19	350	886	6

Division 2

	P	W	D	L	F	A	Pts
Richmond	22	19	2	1	986	410	40
Newcastle	22	19	1	2	1255	346	39
Coventry	22	16	1	5	738	394	33
Bedford	22	15	0	7	720	482	30
London S.	22	11	0	11	549	568	22
Wakefield	22	11	0	11	504	557	22
Roth'ham	22	10	0	12	525	661	20
Moseley	22	9	0	13	492	741	18
Waterloo	22	8	0	14	506	661	16
Blackheath	22	7	0	15	412	641	14
Rugby	22	3	0	19	317	1060	6
Nott'ham	22	2	0	20	344	827	4

Division 3 champions: Exeter
Runners-up: Fylde
Division 4 North champions: Worcester
Division 4 South champions: Newbury

CIS County Championships

Semi-finals

Cornwall	24	Cumbria	38
Somerset	14	Northumberland	10

Final

Cumbria	21	Somerset	13

University Match

Oxford U	7	Cambridge U	23

University Second Teams Match

Oxford U	35	Cambridge U	22

University Under-21 Match

Oxford U	22	Cambridge U	13

Women's University Match

Oxford U	34	Cambridge U	0

British Universities Final

Brunel UC	9	Loughboro' U	8

British Universities Women's Final

St Mark & St John	24	Edinburgh U	20

Hospitals Cup

Guy's & St Thomas'	33	St Mary's	11

Sanyo Cup

Wasps	31	World XV	52

Inter-Services Champions: The Army
Middlesex 7s Winners: Barbarians
Middlesex 7s Plate Winners: Wasps
Shell UK Ltd -Rosslyn Park Schools Sevens
Festival Winners: Canford
Open winners: John Fisher
Colts Winners: Llanhari
Junior Winners: Donhead
Preparatory School Winners: Caldicott
Women's National Cup Final

Richmond	10	Saracens	13

WALES

SWALEC Welsh Challenge Cup

Quarter-finals

Cardiff	57	SW Police	30
Ebbw Vale	17	Bridgend	16
Llanelli	59	Pontypool	17
Neath	24	Swansea	32

Semi-finals

Cardiff	36	Llanelli	26
Ebbw Vale	15	Swansea	26

Final

Cardiff	33	Swansea	26

Division 1

	P	W	D	L	T	B	Pts
Pontypridd	22	20	0	2	124	22	62
Swansea	22	14	0	8	128	22	50
Llanelli	22	16	2	4	111	16	50
Cardiff	22	14	1	7	99	12	41
Bridgend	22	10	1	11	79	10	31
Newport	22	12	2	8	71	5	31
Ebbw Vale	22	12	2	8	50	4	30
Neath	22	10	0	12	74	9	29
Dunvant	22	10	2	10	69	5	27
Caerphilly	22	2	0	20	59	10	14
Treorchy	22	3	0	19	57	4	10
Newbridge	22	4	0	18	45	0	8

Division 2

	P	W	D	L	T	B	Pts
Aberavon	22	16	1	5	107	20	53
Llandovery	22	16	0	6	109	20	52
Cross Keys	22	18	0	4	96	14	50
S Wales Police	22	12	1	9	82	8	33
Pontypool	22	11	2	9	71	9	33
Card Ins	22	10	1	11	86	11	32
Abertillery	22	13	0	9	54	6	32
Bonymaen	22	11	1	10	65	8	31
Maesteg	22	9	0	13	53	7	25
Blackwood	22	7	0	15	44	3	17
Abercynon	22	4	0	18	40	4	10
Ystradgynlais	22	2	0	20	36	2	6

Division 3 champions: Rumney
Runners-up: Merthyr
Division 4 champions: St Peter's
Runners-up: Whitland

SCOTLAND

Tennnets Inter-District Championship

	P	W	D	L	F	A	Pts
Caledonia	3	2	1	0	77	53	5
Glasgow	3	2	0	1	73	57	4
Scot. Borders	3	1	1	1	66	71	3
Edinburgh	3	0	0	3	35	69	0

SRU Tennents Cup Final

Melrose	31	Boroughmuir	23

SRU Tennents Shield Final

Glasgow High -Kelvinside	46	Hawick	18

SRU Tennents Shield Final

Selkirk	23	Biggar	15

Scottish 7s winners

Kelso: Scotland VII
Selkirk: Scotland VII
Gala: Watsonians
Melrose: Kelso
Hawick: Kelso
Jed-Forest: Kelso
Earlston: Kelso
Langholm: Kelso

McEwan's National Leagues

Division 1

	P	W	D	L	F	A	Pts
Melrose	14	14	0	0	582	215	28
Watsonians	14	13	0	1	678	226	24
Currie	14	9	0	5	394	244	18
Boroughmuir	14	6	1	7	391	325	13
Hawick	14	5	0	8	268	397	10
Jed-Forest	14	4	0	10	217	506	8
Heriot's FP	14	3	0	11	224	416	6
Stirling County	14	2	1	11	220	524	5

Division 2

	P	W	D	L	F	A	Pts
Edinburgh Ac.	14	11	0	3	388	187	22
W. of Scot.	14	10	1	3	395	264	21
Dundee HS FP	14	10	1	3	334	205	21
Glasgow High	14	8	1	5	339	265	17
Glasgow Ac.	14	6	0	8	292	339	12
Kelso	14	5	0	9	308	431	10
Gala	14	2	1	11	314	392	5
Biggar	14	2	0	12	187	474	4

Division 3 champions: Kirkcaldy
Runners-up: Kilmarnock
Division 4 champions: Gordonaians
Runners-up: Ayr

IRELAND

Inter-Provincial championship

	P	W	D	L	F	A	Pts
Munster	3	3	0	0	117	92	6
Leinster	3	1	0	2	88	92	2
Ulster	3	1	0	2	81	89	2
St Mary's	3	1	0	2	77	90	2

Senior Provincial Cup winners
Connacht: Galwegians
Leinster: Lansdowne
Munster: Garryowen
Ulster: Ballymena

Insurance Corporation All-Ireland League
Division 1

	P	W	D	L	F	A	Pts
Shannon	13	12	0	1	345	174	24
Lansdowne	13	9	0	4	349	184	18
Terenure Coll.	13	9	0	4	301	179	18
St Mary's	13	8	1	4	305	279	17
Ballymena	13	8	0	5	241	230	16
Cork Const.	13	7	1	5	283	262	15
Blackrock C.	13	7	0	6	288	278	14
Garryowen	13	7	0	6	287	283	14
Y. Munster	13	6	0	7	243	265	12
Dungannon	13	5	0	8	324	344	10
Old Crescent	13	4	0	9	239	281	8
Old Belvedere	13	4	0	9	193	287	8
Old Wesley	13	3	0	10	206	327	6
Instonians	13	1	0	12	173	404	2

Division 2

	P	W	D	L	F	A	Pts
Clontarf	13	11	0	2	329	167	22
Dolphin	13	9	1	3	294	236	19
Bective R.	13	9	0	4	261	146	18
Skerries	13	9	0	4	225	193	18
D. la Sa-Pal'stn	13	6	2	5	285	243	14
Monkstown	13	6	2	5	242	244	14
Univ C. Cork	13	7	0	6	245	273	14
Malone	13	6	0	7	261	255	12
Greystones	13	6	0	7	242	260	12
Sunday's Well	13	5	1	7	282	337	11
Wanderers	13	5	1	7	223	280	11
City of Derry	13	3	0	10	217	303	6
N. of Ire. FC	13	2	1	10	183	324	5
Highfield	13	2	0	11	205	286	42

FRANCE

French Club Championship
Final

Toulouse	23	Agen	16

Yves du Manoir Final

Pau	13	Bourgoin	11

ITALY

Cup Final

Treviso	34	Milan	29

NEW ZEALAND

Championship First Division 1996
Semi-finals

Auckland	59	Otago	18
Counties	46	Canterbury	23

Final

Auckland	46	Counties	15

Ranfurly Shield Holders: Auckland

SOUTH AFRICA

Currie Cup 1996
Semi-finals

Natal	33	Orange FS	20
Transvaal	31	N. Transvaal	21

Final

Natal	33	Transvaal	15

BARBARIAN FC

Opponents		Results
SCOTLAND XV	W	48 – 45
WALES	L	10 – 31
Newport	W	86 – 33
AUSTRALIA	L	12 – 39
Leicester	W	38 – 22
East Midlands	W	72 – 38

Played 6 Won 4 Lost 2

SUPER 12 TOURNAMENT

Final Table

	P	W	D	L	F	A	Pts
Auckland	11	10	1	0	435	283	50
ACT	11	8	0	3	406	291	41
Wellington	11	6	0	5	416	314	34
Natal	11	5	2	4	321	350	30
Gauteng	11	5	1	5	302	346	28
Canterbury	11	5	1	5	272	235	26
Free State	11	5	0	6	301	327	25
N. Transvaal	11	3	3	5	264	342	22
NSW	11	4	0	7	255	296	20
Queensland	11	4	0	7	263	318	20
Waikato	11	4	0	7	272	295	19
Otago	11	3	0	8	299	409	17

Semi-finals

Auckland	55	Natal	36
ACT	33	Wellington	20

Final

Auckland	23	ACT	7

Mission Statement

The Wooden Spoon Society aims to enhance the quality
and prospect of life for children and young persons in the
United Kingdom who are presently disadvantaged either
physically, mentally or socially

Charity Registration No: 326691